Lotus

Illustrated DICTIONARY of INTERNET

Compiled and Edited by:
Tiara Yulu

Lotus
PRESS
4735/22,PrakashDeepBuilding
AnsariRoad,DaryaGanj,
NewDelhi-110002

Lotus *Illustrated*

DICTIONARY *of* INTERNET

ISBN 81 89093 40 1

Published by:
Lotus Press : Publishers & Distributors
Unit No. 220, 2nd Floor, 4735/22,
Prakash Deep Building, Ansari Road, Darya Ganj,
New Delhi- 110002, Ph.: 32903912, 23280047, 09811838000
• E-mail : lotus_press@sify.com www.lotuspress.co.in

Printed at : ***Concept Imprint,*** Delhi
Printed at : **Bharat Offset Works,** New Delhi

PREFACE

The actual term 'Internet' was finally defined in the year 1995. The experts agree that the following language reflects our definition of the term 'Internet'. 'Internet' refers to the global information system that is logically linked together by a globally unique address space based on the Internet Protocol (IP) or its subsequent extensions/follow-ons.

It is able to support communications using the Transmission Control Protocol/Internet Protocol (TCP/IP) suite or its subsequent extensions/follow-ons and/or other IP-compatible protocols. Since 1983 the Internet has accommodated a lot of changes and continues to keep developing. The last two decades has seen the Internet accommodate such things as network LANs and ATM and frame switched services.

The Internet continues to evolve with it becoming available on mobile phones and pagers and possibly on televisions in the future. Internet provides, uses or makes accessible, either publicly or privately, high level services layered on the communications and related infrastructure described herein. The Internet and the World Wide Web are closely related but not the same.

Internet covers a wide variety of topics, such as HTML, e-mail, TCP/IP, search engines, security, viruses, browsers, newsgroups, chat programs, file sharing, FTP, Telnet and more. This Internet Dictionary has been created to help people who have general computer problems, whether they be software, hardware or Internet based. Internet Dictionary is specifically aimed to help Internet users. One can see that the majority of information included will be useful to users anywhere in the English speaking world.

■

HTML coding for a non-breaking space. It is used in HTML between consecutive words on a web page to prevent those two words from being broken apart at the end of a line.

■ .z

a standard file extension for files compressed with UNIX compression. It is also occasionally used in lower case to mean gnu UNIX compression, but .gz is more commonly used for this to avoid confusion.

■ +require or -reject a term or phrase

insert + immediately before a term (no space) to limit search to documents containing a term. Insert - immediately before a term (no space) to exclude documents containing a term. Can be used immediately (no space) before the 'delimiting a phrase'.

Functions partially like basic BOOLEAN LOGIC. If + precedes more than one term, they are required as with Boolean AND. If - is used, terms are excluded as with Boolean AND NOT. If neither + nor - is used, the default if Boolean OR. However, full Boolean logic allows parentheses to group and sequence logical operations and +/- do not.

■ <g>

chat shorthand for 'grin'. Used either to show that you are amused or to say, "Don't take what I said too seriously." The latter usage can prevent misunderstandings!

■ <mtf>

chat shorthand for 'more to follow'. It is also often represented as ... (three dots or ellipsis).

■ <x-delphi>

a special HTML tag for internal Delphi Forums forum promotions. It will display promotions a Forum host sets up in the Forum Control Centre via the Promote menu. The promotions will display in web pages, Message Board welcome screens and messages where the tag and accompanying HTML code are placed.

■ 3-d rendering for the web

software options for 3-D rendering on the web.

■ 56k line

a digital phone-line connection (leased line) capable of carrying 56,000 bits-per-second. At this speed, a Megabyte will take about 3 minutes to transfer. This is 4 times as fast as a 14,400bps modem. See also: **Bandwidth, T-1**.

■ a/s/l

a coded question frequently used in teenage chats. When you see someone type a/s/l, they are asking for your age, sex and location. Use your judgement whether to respond or not.

■ a/v

audio/video marriage of big screen television with movie-theatre-like audio in homes and classrooms.

■ ab roll editing

the transfer of portions of two video sources into one master videotape. For example, one source may be a VCR and the other source a video camera. See also **Video.**

■ ab style switches

analog switchers that are designed to be used in applications whenever multiple computer sources must be connected to a single display device such as a monitor, projector or LCD panel. For example, multiple VGA or SVGA PCs may be connected to a single data projector or PCs and Macs may be connected to a single data projector. Extron carries an extensive line of AB style switches.

■ accelerated/advanced graphics port

a bus specification by that gives 3D graphics cards faster access to main memory than the usual PCI bus. AGP allows scattered data in system memory to be read in bursts. AGP reduces the overall cost by using existing system memory.

■ accelerator board

a hardware electronic board (containing a microprocessor) that can be added to some computers in order to speed up the processing in slow computers. The speed gains are confined to internal calculating and sorting such that no apparent gains are obtained for file management and other busing activities. See also **CPU, Board** and **Bus.**

■ Acceptable Use Policy (AUP)

a formal set of rules that govern how a network may be used. For example, the original NSFnet Acceptable Use Policy forbade non-research use by commercial organisations. AUPs sometimes restrict the type of material that can be made publicly available. Many AUPs ban the transmission of pornographic material. The enforcement of AUPs has historically been very uneven. This was true of the NSFnet AUP: its limitations on commercial activity were so widely ignored that it was finally abandoned in 1994, enabling the development of today's commercial Internet.

■ access number

the telephone number used by a subscriber to dial into an Internet Service Provider or online service.

■ Access Point (AP)

a device connected to the wired local area network that receives and transmits signals to wireless clients, this device must also be connected to the wired LAN if connections to external networks are required.

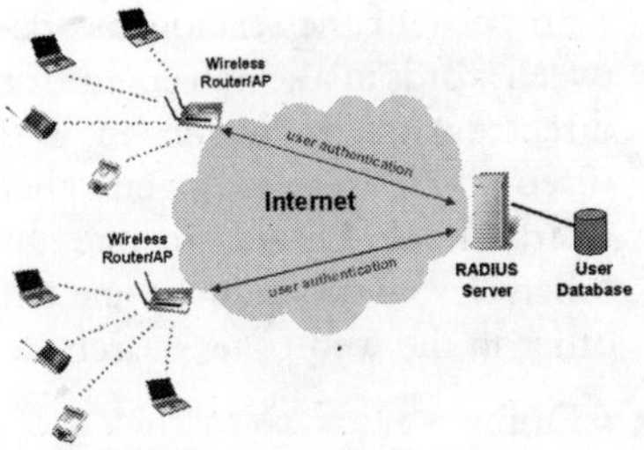

■ ACK

1. acknowledge. Used to confirm one's presence. An appropriate response to ping.
2. when one computer sends a block of data to another over a network, the second computer sends an acknowledgment code back to indicate that the transfer was successful. If there were errors detected in the transmission, the second computer would send a negative acknowledgment (NAK).

■ active video

a video AV standard and open-video architecture that Microsoft Corporation hopes will become the popular standard to replace the Video for Windows (.avi file extension) and Quicktime (.mov file extension) video architecture. Active video attempts to overcome common complaints with its Video for Windows (e.g., limited throughput, poor A/V synchronisation and hardware/software incompatibilities. Also, Active Video will have software MPEG decoding and will cross platforms with Windows, Windows 2000 and Power Macintosh. It will also have an Active Movie filter to play on the Internet via Microsoft's Explorer browser. Whereas Video for Windows was losing out to Apple's Quicktime in popularity, Microsoft's Active Video makes it a closer race between Apple and Microsoft for dominance in the setting of video standards. See also **Video** and **MPEG.**

■ active x

utilities from Microsoft Corporation that combine older Object Linking and Embedding (OLE) and Component Object Model (COM) utilities. Active X is usually coded in Visual Basic and is quite confusing since it is an outgrowth of a complex set of OLE and COM technologies. One of the most widespread applications is to give interactive controls (e.g., ask questions, provide answers, perform computations, push buttons, etc.) to users of Internet Explorer on the web. Therein lies a huge risk as well when computers also have Windows Scripting Host (WSH) utilities using ActiveX. WSH files have a file extension .wsh and are similar to PIF files in older 16-bit applications. Prior to WSH applications, users could browse the web and use e-mail without any worries about virus infections as long as security warnings were heeded about file downloads that run in Microsoft Word, Excel, etc. That is no longer the case if WSH utilities are installed. To avoid such risks, users can either rely upon Netscape products for e-mail and web browsing since Netscape products use Java rather than ActiveX software. If users prefer Microsoft Internet Explorer for web browsing and Microsoft Outlook for e-mail, then they may want to consider adding security barriers to WSH risks. In Internet Explorer you can click on menu choices (View; Internet Options, Security, Custom, Settings) and choose the option to disable 'ActiveX Controls Not Marked as Safe'. Repeat the same procedure for Microsoft Outlook and Outlook Express. You may also want to consider disabling WSH, although you thereby lose the applications relying on WSH utilities.

■ address

there are three types of addresses in common use on the Internet: e-mail addresses, IP addresses and Uniform Resource Locators. See also **e-mail address, IP address, Uniform Resource Locator.**

■ address book

a feature of some e-mail applications that stores names and e-mail addresses in an accessible format.

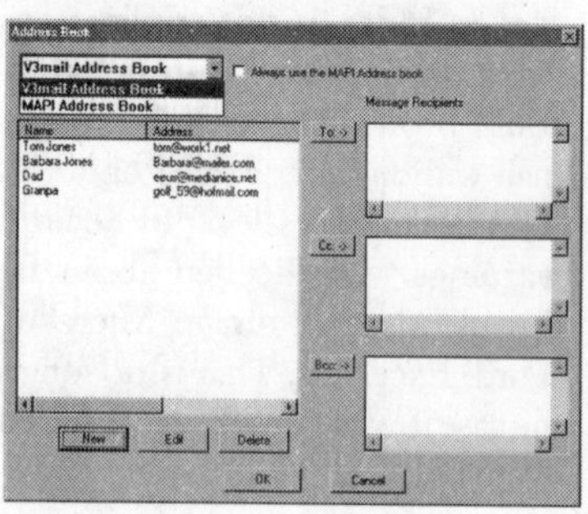

■ adjacency

a property of the relationship between words in a search engine (or directory) query. Search engines often allow users to specify that words should be next to one another or somewhere near one another in the web pages searched.

■ ADN

Advanced Digital Network. Usually refers to a 56K/bps leased-line.

■ ADPCM

Adaptive Differential Pulse Code Modulation. Audio waveform sampling that records the difference between samples is recorded rather than the actual values. This increases fidelity with lower resolution than conventional PCM.

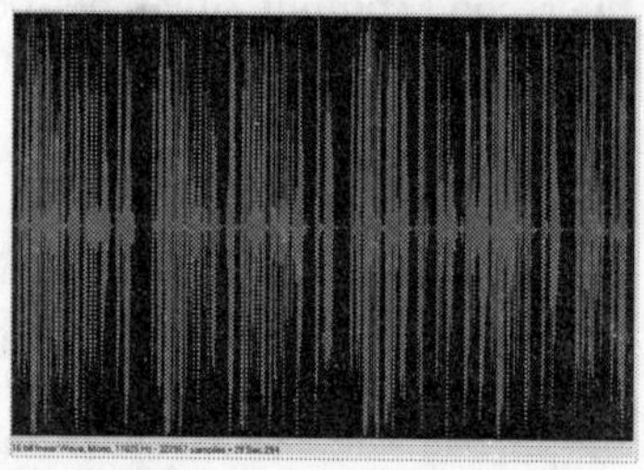

■ ADSL

Asymmetric Digital Subscriber Line. New technology to carry high-speed data over ordinary phone lines. It is up to 70 times as fast as a 28.8 modem and can be used concurrently with voice over the same line. It is gradually being offered to homes commercially now. It is called 'asymmetric' because download speeds to the subscriber are faster than upload speeds from the subscriber.

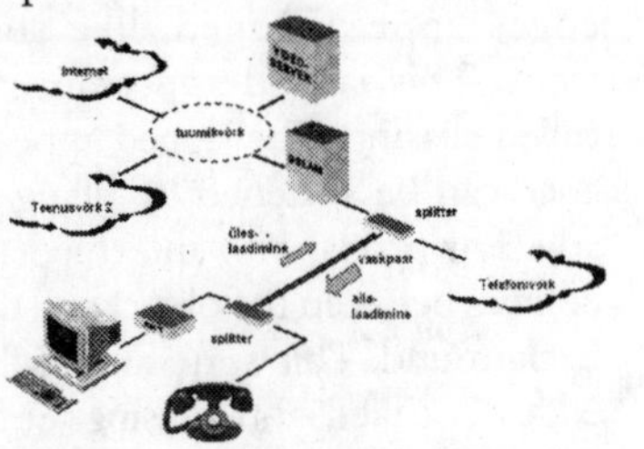

■ Advanced Research Projects Agency (ARPA)

agency of the U. S. Department of Defence that promotes exploratory research in areas that carry long term promise for military applications. ARPA funded the major packet switching experiments in the United States that led to the Internet, particularly the ARPANET.

■ adware

any software which serves banner ads or pop-up ads to you while in use. It is sometimes installed in freeware or shareware, which you download from the net and provides one more channel for advertisers to reach you. Some adware will also track your files, net usage and software and report it back to advertisers to help them channel relevant ads to you.

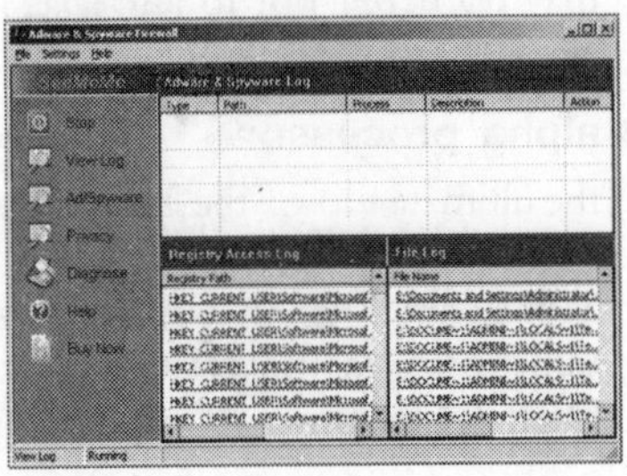

■ AFK

chat abbreviation for Away From Keyboard.

■ agent name delivery

the process of sending search engine spiders to a tailored page, yet directing your visitors to what you want them to see. This is done using server side includes (or other dynamic content techniques). SSI, for example, can be used to deliver different content to the client depending on the value of HTTP_USER_AGENT. Most normal browser software packages have a user agent string which starts with 'Mozilla' (coined from Mosaic and Godzilla). Most search engine spiders have specific agent names, such as 'Gulliver', 'Infoseek sidewinder', 'Lycos spider' and 'Scooter'. By switching on the value of HTTP_USER_AGENT (a process known as agent detection), different pages can be presented at the same URL, so that normal visitors will never see the page submitted to search engines (and vice versa).

In practise this is somewhat simplistic. Some search engines pretend to be 'plain mozilla' browsers to prevent use of agent name delivery. Effective use of agent name delivery can be very difficult and may not even work.

How do you spot agent name delivery at work? This is quite difficult, as the owners of web pages using agent name delivery can control what you see! You may be able to guess that a page is using this technique if it appears to be indexed incorrectly or the title or description don't match the page you see, but this could also have been achieved by switching pages after the relevant search engine has indexed it. If you really want to see the search engines' tailored version of a page, write a program (e.g. a Perl script) to retrieve the URL with HTTP_USER_AGENT set to each of the strings used by the search engine spiders. If agent name delivery is in use, one or more of the retrieved pages will be different to the others!

■ AIFF

Audio Interchange File Format. A common audio file format originally for Macs, but used with other systems, too.

■ aix

an IBM version of the Unix operating system. It will run on PCs with 386 or higher chips and on workstations and mainframes. See also **Unix**.

■ algorithm

procedure, a crypto algorithm defines a particular procedure for encrypting or decrypting data. Specific algorithms include DES, IDEA, RC4, SKIPJACK.

■ aliasing, anti-aliasing

pictures on your computer monitor are made up of square pixels. When the edge of a solid coloured object in a GIF image is a diagonal or curved line and it is displayed against a contrasting colour, the edges appear jagged, like stair steps. This jagged appearance is called aliasing. The jagged appearance can be softened by filling in adjacent pixels with intermediate colours between the object and the background. This softening of the edges is called anti-aliasing. Software like PhotoShop can apply anti-aliasing for you automatically. It is often the default setting.

One problem with anti-aliasing GIF images is that it increases the number of colours used, necessarily increasing the file size. You must decide whether quick loading or smoothed edges serves your needs better.

A second problem can occur when you create transparent GIFs. If the edges are anti-aliased against a different colour background than the background it will be displayed against, the intermediate colour pixels will be the wrong colour and a halo effect occurs around the image. Make sure that when you anti-alias transparent GIFs, that you do it against the final background colour. If you are using a tiled background image where the background colour changes, you may do better not to anti-alias at all.

■ alpha processor

the ultimate top-of-the line processor for PCs that uses DEC's 21064 chip. The 'Alpha-based' systems such as the DECpc from Digital Equipment Corporation claims it is the fastest system available for Windows 2000.

■ alpha test

in software development, an early stage of testing by in-house personnel to identify bugs in the program. It usually involves systematically trying out all of a program's functions. Compare with beta test.

■ alt

1. a top-level category of 'alternative' USENET newsgroups. These unmoderated newsgroups can be started by anyone with the time, equipment and expertise. The alt hierarchy covers perhaps the widest variety of topics ranging from the informative to the bizarre and from the politically radical to the explicitly sexual.
2. the Alt key on the keyboard of IBM PC compatibles, typically used in conjunction with other keys.

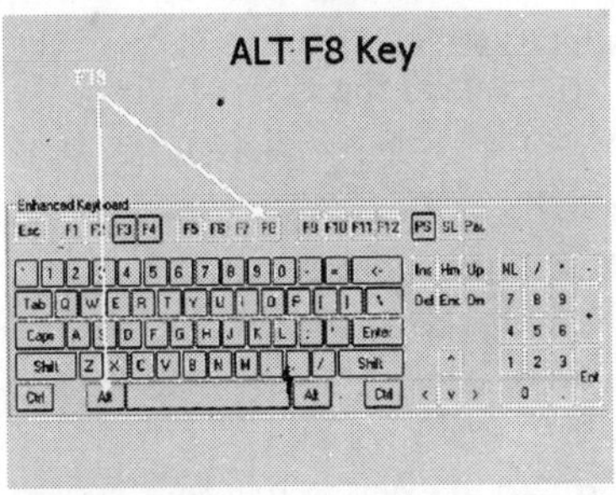

■ Altavista

a popular search engine with the largest database on the web, indexing more than 140 million pages. Its main URL is http://www.altavista.com. Until 1998, this search engine provided the search facility for Yahoo. Altavista indexes all the words in a web page and new pages are normally added to the database fairly quickly, within a couple of working days. You are asked to submit just the main page of your site. The Altavista spider will then explore your site and index a representative sample of the pages. Some problems with spamming have been noticed. The use of keyword meta tags is penalised. Altavista places various alternative options before its search results, including suggested questions (using the Ask Jeeves service), RealNames. Paid entries are beginning to appear at the start of the search results.

■ America Online

the commercial AOL network (800-827-6364) that 'remains the hottest, easiest-to-use and most interesting of the services' according to Mossberg (1994a). AOL offers Time Magazine, the Chigago Tribune and other news and television network options. New services to educators online include an American Federation of Teachers online doctoral program from the Electronic University Network and the Forum on Technology in Education and Training (FORUM-TET).

■ American National Standards Institute (ANSI)

organisation that endorses and publishes standards for various industries.

Amiga

a video computing hardware/software desktop workstation formerly manufactured and marketed by Commodore International based on Motorola microprocessors. Amiga workstations became a widely popular option in conjunction with NewTek's Video Toaster software for home and office videotape productions. Amiga developed its own operating system called Amiga DOS. A major drawback is that as a computer it does not communicate (i.e., its files are not readable) on more popular Apple, PC and Unix operating systems. For example, it can neither read MS-DOS files into its operating system nor write out MS-DOS files. It is far less of a competitor for digital computers and networking than for analog video computers such as Mac Video. The new Amiga workstations became aggressive low-priced competitors to Silicon Graphics and Sun workstations for 3D animation rendering for broadcast quality video. The future of the Amiga is clouded by the 1994 declaration of bankruptcy and subsequent liquidation of the former Commodore International Corporation. At this juncture it is uncertain whether another manufacturer will take over all Amiga technologies and patents. NewTek Inc. (800-847-6111) now sells workstations for its Video Toaster software formerly used in Amiga computers. The Amiga and NewTek workstations compete with Apple AV and SGI competitors, but these options should not be confused with the more extensive concepts of network video servers.

AMPS (Advanced Mobile Phone Service)

this basic analog cellular service in the United States and South America typically operates at 800 MHz and uses FDMA transmission technology. With AMPS, when one person grabs a segment of frequency for a call, nobody else within the cell can use it. Digital cellular technologies offer ways for carriers to allow more calls in a cell, using the same amount of bandwidth.

analog

see **video.**

anchor

synonymous with hyperlinks, anchor refers to non-linear links among documents. Or more simply put, it's the word or phrase that can be selected to connect to another page resource.

anchor colour

the colour on a browser screen that represents the anchor tag (navigation item) colours. The reason so many are blue is that blue is often the default colour in browser software. This colour can be changed to any combination of red, green and blue. The ability to change these colours at the reader level complicates choice of colour at the authoring level.

■ **animated gif**

a GIF graphic file, which consists of two or more images shown in a timed sequence to give the effect of motion.

■ **animation**

time-phased moving graphic images that give the impression of motion such as in motion picture cartoons or videographic movements of objects about the screen. Several frames show a progression of movement and thereby simulate movement.

■ **annotations**

personal notes you can attach to the documents you have saved in your Web browser. The notes are available to you whenever the document is viewed.

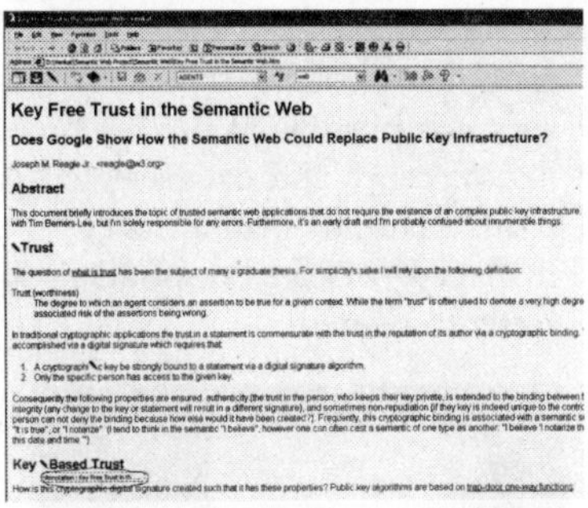

■ **anonymous FTP**

a service that allows free public access to archived documents, files and programs via the File Transfer Protocol (FTP). It's not necessary to have a user ID and password when logging into an anonymous FTP site. The user ID 'anonymous' bypasses local security checks, often e-mail addresses serve as courtesy passwords. The picture shows an

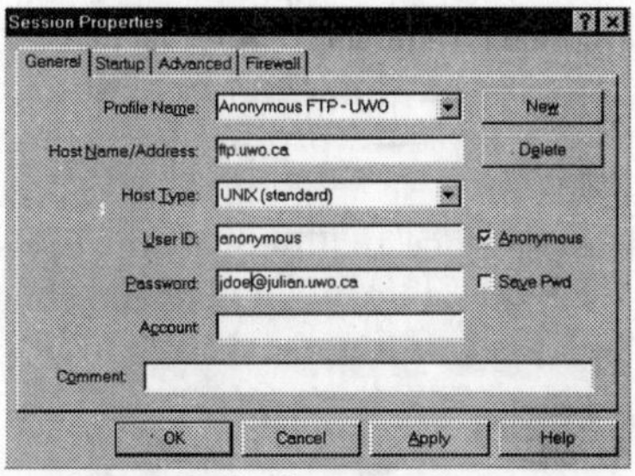

example of a how to log on to a network using the anonymous FTP.

■ **ANSI x9.17**

ANSI standard for secret key exchange using the DES algorithm.

■ **anti-replay**

security feature that detects when a message on the network has been received more than once. This applies stronger restrictions on duplicate packets than are enforced by typical networking protocols that don't anticipate messages being replayed maliciously.

■ **API**

Application Program Interface. An interface by which an application program accesses operating system. An API can also provide an interface between a high level language and lower level utilities and services, which were written without consideration for the calling conventions supported by compiled languages. Netscape Corporation and Microsoft both provide APIs called NSAPI and ISAPI that essentially extend their web servers and it provides developers a way to put application code actually within the web server. This means that you don't have to start up a separate process each time one of these applications is called. And, since that application is always running, it can maintain connections to the database.

■ applet

a Java program which is designed to run only on a web page. To use an applet on a web page, you would specify the name of the applet and the size (length and width—in pixels) that the applet can utilise. When the web page is accessed, the browser downloads the applet from a server and runs it on the user's machine (the client). Applets differ from applications in that they are governed by a strict security protocol. For example, even though applets run on the client, they cannot read or write data onto the client's machine. Additionally, applets are further restricted so that they can only read and write data from the same domain that they are served from.

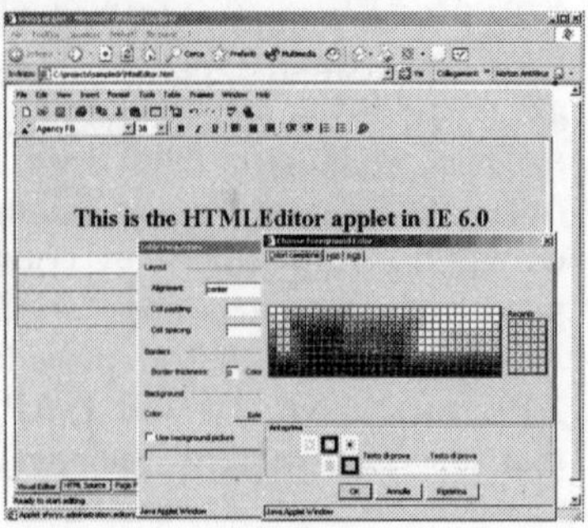

■ application

a self-contained program that performs a well-defined set of tasks under user control, as opposed to a system program. Web browsers, mail readers and FTP clients are examples of applications commonly used on the Internet.

■ application encryption

cryptographic functions built into the communications protocols for a specific application, like e-mail. Examples include PEM, PGP and SHTTP.

■ application server

server software that manages one or more other software packages in a way that makes the features of the managed software available over a network, usually to a *Web* server. By having a piece of software manage other software packages it is possible to use resources like memory and database access more efficiently than if each of the managed packages responded directly to requests.

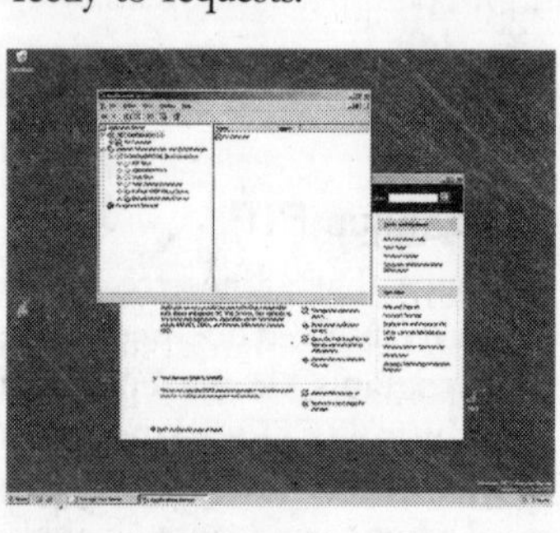

■ application software

software that provides a service to a user, as opposed to lower level software that makes useful services possible.

■ archie

a tool (software) for finding files stored on anonymous FTP sites. You need to know the exact file name or a substring of it. By 1999 *Archie* had been almost completely replaced by web-based search engines. Back when FTP was the main way people moved files over the Internet archie was quite popular.

■ architextspider

the name of the Excite search engine's spider.

■ archive

1. a storage repository for software, data or other materials to be saved and preserved.
2. a technique of combining multiple files into a single file to enable easier backup, handling or transmission. Some of the software programs used to archive files are PKZIP, WinZip, Stuffit and tar. Files with the following extensions are likely to be archived: sea, tar, taz, taZ, tgz and zip.

■ ARPANET

forerunner of the Internet created by the United States military during the cold war. ARPANET was designed by its founders to be a military command and control centre that could withstand nuclear attack. ARPANET's founders designed it so that authority was distributed over a large number of geographically dispersed computers. This concept of a computer network with distributed authority is the basis of the Internet. Theoretically, if 90% of the Internet were destroyed by nuclear attack, the remaining servers would be able to continue on—assuming that all life on Earth were not obliterated. Over time the defence-oriented purpose of the Internet was broadened to include research and development, universities and education and recently, commerce.

■ art

a graphics format used on AOL. Plug-ins are available for non-AOL browsers to view graphics with a .art extension.

■ Artificial Intelligence (AI)

a branch (usually called AI/Expert Systems) of computer science, mathematics, psychology and systems engineering that attempts to make computer 'decision making' more like human decision making and to aid or replace human decision makers with machines. Expert systems attempt to utilise the skills, knowledge and decision evaluation processes of human experts. For example, computers now aid physicians in diagnosing diseases and computer-guided laser rockets virtually replace human guidance decisions. AI failed to live up to its early expectations when it was believed that AI computers would never fail to win at chess and language translators would soon be put out of work by computers. However, applications of AI have been taking place and computers can now play very good chess to a point where they occasionally beat even the grand masters.

■ ASCII

American Standard Code for Information Interchange. Computer character set (text and symbols) that enables transfer of text and data between different computing systems. This international standard provides only very plain text without options for font modifications. For example, files from word processors such as Microsoft Word, Word Perfect and Word Star often cannot be imported to hypertext or hypermedia software without conversion to ASCII code (most word processors will change files to ASCII 'text' files). The downside is that nearly all formatting and font variations are lost in ASCII conversions such that imported ASCII text may have to be re-formatted line by line and altered for font preferences. Very few software alternatives have 'filters' that import word processor files directly without having to convert to ASCII codes, although many are now adding rich-text format (RTF) utilities. In hypertext authoring, choice of a hypertext software option should include a question concerning whether 'filters' are available for avoidance of ASCII text conversions. See also **ANSI, Internet messaging** and **rich-text format.**

■ ASCII art

artwork composed entirely of ASCII characters used as lines and shapes, not as characters with meanings. The simplest ASCII art is the simple smiley faces, but at the other end of the scale, they can be large, elaborate pictures.

■ ASCII file

ASCII files are those that only use the 128 characters that can be encoded with 7 binary digits. This means that most text files are ASCII files. Word-processed files, which include special characters and control codes are usually encoded with 8 binary digits. Some Internet protocols only support 7-bit text, such as simple mailers and newsgroups. Because of this, ways have been developed to encode binary files into ASCII form. The most common of these are uuencode and binhex, the latter for Macintosh files, primarily. Two more examples of 7-bit file systems are postscript (.ps files) and TeX (.tex files), which are word processing systems that allow encoding of complex information in 7-bit form. Common extensions for ASCII files are .txt, .uue, .xxe, .hqx, .ps and .tex. Also files with names like README or index are almost always text files. The .doc extension may be text or may be 8-bit and you need to know more about it to be sure.

■ ask jeeves

a meta search engine which can be asked questions in English. This service is also in use at Altavista. http://www.askjeeves.com.

ASP

1. Application Service Provider that provides individuals or enterprises access over the Internet to applications and related services. This service is sometimes referred to as 'apps-on-tap'. Early applications include: Remote access serving for the users of an enterprise. An off-premises local area network to which mobile users can be connected, with a common file server. Specialised applications that would be expensive to install and maintain within your own company or on your own computer.
2. Active Server Pages. ASP script extensions contain either Visual Basic or Jscript code. When a browser requests an ASP page, the Web server generates a page with HTML code and sends it back to the browser. So ASP pages are similar to CGI scripts, but they enable Visual Basic programmers to work with familiar tools. This is a page that performs customised 'applications' services. Business transactions (such as billings and collections) can even be managed by the applications server.

aspect ratio

the ratio of the horizontal to vertical size of the screen. Some monitors display rectangular pixels, which can make the picture or image appear stretched. Software that allows images to be resized and changed with respect to aspect ratios greatly facilitates authoring. Otherwise, images have to be transported to other software for such changes and then transported back in a cumbersome process that makes authors grateful when aspect ratios and image sizes can be modified without such difficulties. Macromedia Director is one of the very few hypermedia authoring systems that has a utility for changing the scale and aspect ratios of imported bitmap pictures as well as rotating and inverting such pictures.

assessment

the evaluation of the efficiency and effectiveness of technology on attitudes and performance. There are various assessment scales such as the Computer Attitude Scale, the Computer Anxiety Rating Scale and the Computer Self-Efficacy Scale. Assessment is very difficult because no matter how good the findings are in an empirical study, the relevance of those findings quickly falls away due to constantly emerging technologies that are significantly better than older technologies used in the study.

asymmetric algorithm

a crypto algorithm that uses different keys for encryption and decryption, most often a public key algorithm.

asynchronous connection

the type of connection a modem makes over a phone line, this connection is not synchronised by a mutual timing signal or clock.

■ **Asynchronous Learning Networks (ALN)**

ALN networks of education and training modules or courses where students learn in self-paced online pedagogy in contrast to synchronised presentations in traditional classrooms or electronic classrooms. Synchronous education in a scheduled sequence of classes will face serious new competition of asynchronous education distributed on networks where students learn and communicate most any day and most any time of day and study at their own paces. In addition, asynchronous courses may schedule synchronous virtual online meetings of subsets of students or entire classes of students. Networked courses may thus be synchronous and asynchronous, although the technical learning components are largely asynchronous.

■ **ATM**

1. Automatic Teller Machines for banks.

2. Asynchronous Transfer Mode switching in networks. The high-speed ATM networks allow transmission of video, audio and data over local and worldwide networks.

■ **attached file**

a file that is embedded into an e-mail message.

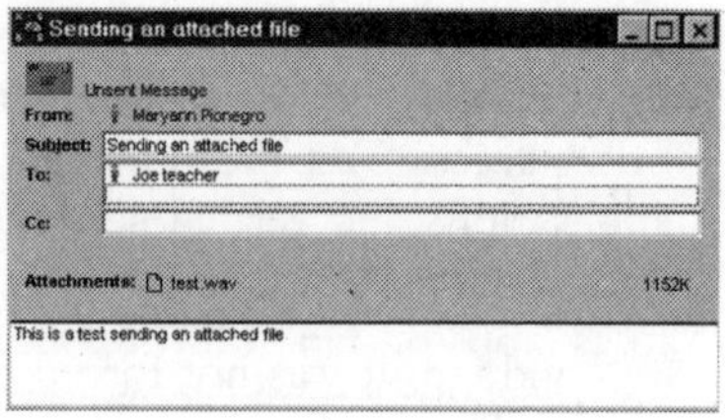

■ **AU sounds**

this is an audio format developed for Sun workstations and often used to distribute sound clips via the Web.

■ **audio**

voice, music and other sounds recorded and stored in analog or digital form. The term RealAudio refers to a helper-app (plug-in) that allows WWW users to hear audio files in real time. Options for creating and playing digital audio Java applets are reviewed in deCarmo (1996). Options for converting written text into audio are given in Text reading.

■ **audio board**

see **sound board.**

■ **audio card**

see **sound board.**

■ **audio conversion to text**

see **text reading.**

■ **audio on the Internet**

see **Internet audio and video.**

■ **audio streaming**

see **web streaming.**

■ authentication

the process of verifying that a particular name really belongs to a particular entity.

■ authenticity

the ability to ensure that the given information was in fact produced by the entity whose name it carries and that it was not forged or modified.

■ authoring

developing (writing of text, recording of audio, importing of video, inserting graphics, etc.) hypertext and hypermedia learning, entertainment and reference materials.

■ authoring software

this term refers to software that enables the creation of multimedia or hypertext documents and presentations.

■ AVI

Audio Video Interleaved. Digitised video files (with audio tracks) that satisfy MPC standards for Video for Windows playback. The Media Player (mplayer.exe) file that is included in Windows operating systems runs AVI files. Most PC video capture boards will convert analog video into AVI files. The AVI standard from Microsoft's Video for Windows is giving way to Microsoft's newer Active Video architecture.

■ b2b

business to business. A mode of conducting business between two or more companies over the Internet, rather than more traditional modes such as telephone, mail and face to face.

■ b2c

business to consumer. Another business model over the Internet.

■ back / forward

buttons in most browsers' Tool Button Bar, upper left. 'Back' returns you to the document previously viewed. 'Forward' goes to the next document, after you go back. If it seems like the 'Back' button does not work, check if you are in a new Netscape window, some Web pages are programmed to open a new window when you click on some links. Each window has its own short-term search 'History'. If this does not work, use 'Go' to select the page you want (some Web pages are programmed to disable 'Back').

■ backbone

a high-speed line or series of connections that forms a major pathway within a network. The term is relative as a backbone in a small *network* will likely be much smaller than many non-backbone lines in a large network.

■ back-end

the final stage in a process or a task not apparent to the user. A common usage is in a compiler. A compiler's back-end generates machine language and performs optimisations specific to the machine's architecture. The term can also be used in the context of

Open System Interconnect (OSI) network applications. A standard for layering of protocols (protocol stack) to implement it was developed in 1978 as a framework for international standards in heterogeneous computer network architecture. The architecture is split between seven layers (lowest to highest):
1. physical layer
2. data link layer
3. network layer
4. transport layer
5. session layer
6. presentation layer
7. application layer
Generally, each layer uses the layer immediately below it and provides a service to the layer above in a 'back ended' way. In the third generation of network computing, web servers perform back-end database computing where it's controlled and managed. But third generation computing takes advantage of the new interactive server/client interactive technology like Sun's Java and Microsoft's ActiveX/CORBA. Users on the client side want to interact in various ways such as perform sensitivity (what-if) type of analysis.

■ bailey the switcher

attacks network traffic by modifying the contents of other people's messages.

■ bait-and-switch

the provision of one page for a search engine or directory and a different page for other user agents at the same URL. Various methods can be used, e.g. Agent Name Delivery or IP Delivery.

■ bandwidth

1. the amount of information or data that can be sent over a network connection in a given period of time. Bandwidth is usually stated in bits per second (bps), kilobits per second (kbps) or megabits per second (mps).
2. the technical meaning is generalised in hacker slang. Individuals are said to be 'high bandwidth' if they are able to process large volumes of information in short periods of time.

■ bang address

an old system of mail addressing in UUCP networks, where the successive routing addresses were followed by exclamation points (also known as bangs) and the addressee was the last element.

■ barfmail

repeated bounce messages, usually due to mail server or gateway errors, which cause significant annoyance.

■ BASIC

acronym for Beginners All-purpose Symbolic Instructional Code. An easy-to-learn, highly flexible computer language invented at Dartmouth University. Different versions of BASIC run on various operating systems. Since each version has its own peculiar quirks, a BASIC program written in one version may not be compatible with another version.

The 'Hello World!' program in BASIC:

10 PRINT 'Hello World!'
20 END

■ baud

in common usage the baud rate of a *modem* is how many *bits* it can send or receive per second. Technically, baud is the number of times per second that the carrier signal shifts value - for example a 1200 bit-per-second modem actually runs at 300 baud, but it moves 4 bits per baud (4 x 300= 1200 bits per second).

■ baud rate

a nearly obsolete term for transmission rates synonymous in early, simple systems with bits per second. In faster, more complex systems of encoding and transmitting data, the term loses its simple meaning and has fallen into disuse (and frequent misuse). See **baud**.

■ Baudot code

the Baudot code, used by early teleprinters, represents letters, numbers and symbols in five-character binary codes, which includes shifts to increase the number of characters beyond 32.

■ BBL

chat shorthand for 'Be Back Later'.

■ BBS

Bulletin Board System. A computerised meeting and announcement system that allows people to carry on discussions, upload and download files and make announcements without the people being connected to the computer at the same time. There are many thousands (millions?) of BBS's around the world, most are very small, running on a single IBM clone PC with 1 or 2 phone lines. Some are very large and the line between a BBS and a system like CompuServe gets crossed at some point, but it is not clearly drawn.

■ bcc

abbreviation for Blind Carbon Copy. To bcc: an e-mail message to someone is to send him a copy of the e-mail message without the knowledge of the person to whom the e-mail message is addressed.

■ beta test

in software development, a stage of testing where the program is tried out with a selected trial audience to find and correct bugs, usually people of similar backgrounds to those expected to use the software. Check out Delphi's Beta Test Forum. Compare to alpha test.

■ BFN

chat shorthand for 'Bye For Now'.

■ binary

binary means the use of only two values, zero and one, in encoding data. All digital computers primarily use some form of binary encoding, such as 8 or 16 or 32 binary digits at a time. Characters that you see on screen or type with your keyboard are normally encoded with 8 binary digits. For example, the binary value for the letter A is 01000001.

■ binary files

binary files are files that include up to 256 different characters and are encoded by 8 binary digits (bits) for each character. Simple text or ASCII files only use 128 different characters and can be encoded by 7 binary digits. Examples of binary files are most programs, most word- processed files, most graphics files and most sound files. If you don't know a file is ASCII, it is probably a binary file.

■ BINHEX

BINary HEXadecimal. It is a method for converting non-text files (non-ASCII) into ASCII. This is needed because Internet e-mail can only handle ASCII. See also **ASCII**

■ bit

a contraction of binary digit, a bit is the smallest unit of information that a computer can hold. Eight bits is equivalent to a byte. The speed at which bits are transmitted or bit rate is usually expressed as bits per second or bps.

■ bitmap

a graphic which is defined by specifying the colours of dots or pixels which make up the picture. Also known as raster graphics. Common types of bitmap graphics are GIF, JPEG, Photoshop, PCX, TIFF, Macintosh Paint, Microsoft Paint, BMP, PNG, FAX formats and TGA. See **vector graphics** for a different type of graphic and **metafiles** for a combination of the two types.

■ BITNET

(Because It's Time Network) - A network of educational sites separate from the Internet, but e-mail is freely exchanged between BITNET and the Internet. *Listservs*, the most popular form of e-mail discussion groups originated on BITNET. BITNET machines are IBM VMS machines and the network is probably the only international network that is shrinking.

■ bits per second (bps)

measurement of the data transmission for a modem or network.

■ blog or web log

a blog is basically a journal that is available on the *web*. The activity of updating a blog is 'blogging' and someone who keeps a blog is a 'blogger'. Blogs are typically updated daily using software that allows people with little or no technical background to update and maintain the blog. Postings on a blog are almost always arranged in chronological order with the most recent additions featured most prominently.

■ bmp

bitmap graphics files that are accessible through Windows Paintbrush and most other PC graphics software.

■ **bnc, bnc connector**

short for BayoNet Connector or Baby N Connector or Bayonet Neill-Concelman (for the inventors Paul Neill and Carl Concelman who developed the similar N and C connectors separately and the BNC and TNC connectors together). It is also sometimes called a British Naval Connector, although the origin is questionable. A twist-and-lock connector for coaxial cable, BNC connectors are used for electronic equipment and LANs and permit frequencies into the gigaHertz ranges.

■ **board**

a hardware component that fits into the expansion slot of a computer unit and expands the capabilities of the computer. A board can enable the computer to communicate with an external hardware device, such as a CD-ROM. Alternate terms are card, expansion card, interface card, interface board.

■ **bookmark/favorites**

way in Netscape to store in your computer direct links to sites you wish to return to. The equivalent in Internet Explorer (IE) is called a 'Favorite'. To create a bookmark in Netscape, click on 'Bookmarks', then 'Add Bookmark'. Or left-click on and drag the little bookmark icon (in Netscape 4.6 and higher, to the right of the word Bookmark) to the place you want a new bookmark filed. To visit a bookmarked site, click on 'Bookmarks' and select the site from the list. The equivalent in Internet Explorer to Netscape's Bookmarks is called 'Favorites.'

You can download a bookmark file to diskette and install it on another computer. To do this in Netscape, select 'Bookmarks', then 'Edit Bookmarks', then, in the File menu, select Save As. To do this in IE, select from the main browser tool bar File, then Import and Export... and follow directions for exporting to a file. Import (part of the same IE program) allows you to bring a Netscape Bookmark file into IE as Favorites.

■ **boolean logic**

way to combine terms using 'operators' such as 'AND', 'OR', 'AND NOT' and sometimes 'NEAR'. AND requires all terms appear in a record. OR retrieves records with either term. AND NOT excludes terms. Parentheses may be used to sequence operations and group words. Always enclose terms joined by OR with parentheses. See **+require or -reject term** and **fuzzy and.**

■ **boolean search**

a method of searching for information in databases that combines search terms with the operators AND or, NOT and parentheses.

■ **boot**

to start up or reset a computer. When a computer is booted, a bootstrap routine is automatically executed that looks for and loads the operating system. A cold boot is when the computer is powered up from an off state. A warm boot occurs when an already turned on computer is rebooted.

■ **bot**

short for robot, a program designed to search the Internet looking for information. A common use of bots is the variously named spiders, worms and crawlers that support search engines by following links from site to site and within a site to dig out information to be indexed by the search engine.

■ **bounce message**

a notification message returned to sender indicating that an e-mail message could not be delivered. Usually the message is automatically generated by the Postmaster at the recipient's site, sometimes with an indication of what went wrong. The most common problem is an incorrect address, but sometimes e-mail sent via the Internet fails for no apparent reason.

■ **bozo filter**

a feature of some e-mail and newsgroup reader applications that screens out incoming messages from those whose correspondence in not valued.

■ **bps**

abbreviation for bits per second. A measurement of the number of bits of information that can be sent over a network connection.

■ **BRB**

chat shorthand for 'Be Right Back'.

■ **bridge**

a device that connects different LANs so a node on one LAN can communicate with a node on another LAN.

■ **broadband**

network transmission capacity that greatly exceeds capacity required for voice transmission over traditional telephone cables. Broadband networks may have dedicated portions for audio, video and data or they may allow for capacity switching.

■ **browse**

to follow links in a page, to shop around in a page, exploring what's there, a bit like window shopping. The opposite of browsing a page is searching it. When you search a page, you find a search box, enter terms and find all occurrences of the terms throughout the site. When you browse, you have to guess which words on the page pertain to your interests. Searching is usually more efficient, but sometimes you find things by browsing that you might not find because you might not think of the 'right' term to search by.

■ **browser**

software that will load and display a web page. A browser interprets the HTML or XML code from the web page files, executes embedded scripts and programs, provides encryption/ decryption for security where needed, displays graphics (except text-only browsers), plays music and video and provides links to related pages. Browsers are purportedly based on standards developed by the World Wide Web Consortium and recognised by the Internet Engineering Task Force. The major browser software developers participate in these organisations, but each of them also builds in their own proprietary codes, whether or not approved by the organisations. These differences in browsers create a challenge for web page developers. The principle browsers are Netscape, Microsoft Internet Explorer, Opera, Mosaic and the text-only Lynx.

■ browser war

a catch phrase that refers to the battles between Netscape and Microsoft for dominance of the web browser market. Both sides seek to maximise their product's marketshare and mindshare in cyberspace. The battles are marked by short product development cycles, publicity campaigns, provocative public statements, appeals for federal intervention and a general desire to crush the other side.

■ BTDT

chat slang for 'Been there, done that'.

■ BTW

abbreviation for 'By the Way' used in e-mail, newsgroup and chat communication.

■ bucket brigade

attack against public key exchange in which the attacker substitutes their own public key for the requested public key. Also called Man-in-Middle attack.

■ buffer underrun

a common error where the data stream being fed from the CD-R's cache buffer falls behind the laser doing the writing. See also **CD-R.**

■ bug

a problem with computer software or hardware that causes it to malfunction or crash.

■ bulletin board system

a service dedicated to a specific topic where users post messages that are read by others. It is a computer or computers that offer dial-in communication, which offers users the ability to send e-mail, use news-groups and sometimes access the Internet.

■ **bus topology**

a physical layout of a LAN where all nodes are connected to a single cable.

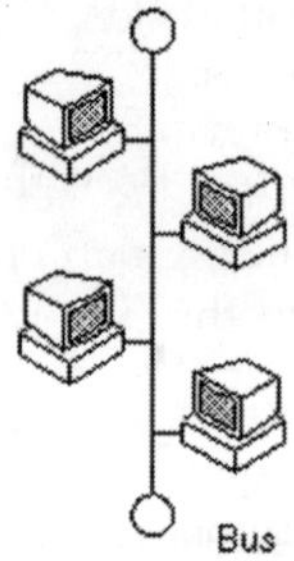

■ **bypass**

flaw in a security device that allows messages to go around the security mechanisms. Crypto bypass refers to flaws that allow plaintext to leak out.

■ **byte**

a set of Bits that represent a single character. Usually there are 8 Bits in a Byte, sometimes more, depending on how the measurement is being made.

■ **C**

the name of a sophisticated computer language commonly used for the creation of professional-grade applications. C is distinguished from other computer languages by its usage of pointers, variables that point at locations in memory. It was invented by Dennis Ritchie in the early 1970s.

This is the C version of 'Hello World':

```
#include 'stdio.h'
main() {
printf('Hello World!'); }
```

■ **C++**

a computer language based on C that uses objected-oriented programming design principles.

■ **cache**

browsers such as Netscape and Microsoft Internet Explorer hold copies of recently visited web files, both HTML and binary files, in disk memory. This disk memory space is called the cache. It offers the advantage of much quicker loading when files are stored on disk than when they must be transferred from the web. The disadvantage is that it will sometimes show you an old version of a file from your disk when a newer one is available on the web. Some large Internet service providers also cache frequently visited sites and feed them to you from their own cache when you try to visit them. You can set the size of the cache to meet the needs of your own system and the speed of your connection. You can also set how often your system will check back to see if there is a newer version. There is a definite trade-off between faster load times and the risk of seeing outdated material. Usually, you can check for a newer version by using the Refresh or Reload selections in your browser. If something looks out of date, always try the Refresh or Reload before trying other things.

Sometimes files in cache can become corrupted and cause problems for your browser. When you have problems diagnosing freeze-ups where they didn't occur before, one of the easy solutions to try is to delete your cache and see if it solves the problems.

■ Cascading Style Sheets (CSS)

Cascading Style Sheets is a technique built into version 4.0 and later browsers that support styles for pages. For example, you can set up styles for fonts and page layouts that will apply automatically to pages developed under a particular style you develop. This technique is useful, but the present version browsers from Netscape and Microsoft are quite different in their implementation and what works with one is not likely to work for the other. For compatibility, care has to be taken to use common elements.

■ capstone

integrated circuit containing crypto functions for e-mail applications using the SKIPJACK cipher and the Escrowed Encryption Standard. It failed to find a customer base and is no longer manufactured.

■ capture

a NetWare utility program used to redirect output from a printer port on the workstation to a network printer.

■ card

see **board.**

■ cascade

a series of reply posts to a USENET message, each adding a trivial or nonsense theme to the corpus of previous replies. Some consider this art, there is a USENET newsgroup devoted to propagating this self-expressive form (alt cascade).

■ CASE

Computer Assisted Software Engineering tools for automating information systems design and programming. The CASE tools are listed and extensively explained various web sites.

■ case sensitive

capital letters (upper case) retrieve only upper case. Most search tools are not case sensitive or only respond to initial capitals, as in proper names. It is always safe to key all lower case (no capitals), because lower case will always retrieve upper case.

■ castanet

see **webcasting**.

■ casting

see **webcasting**.

■ CAT

that subset of CAL that entails Computer Aided Teaching. This subset is restricted to software designed for authoring and/or delivery of learning materials in a classroom or on line in a computer network or teleconference in which the instructor is present and using the CAT materials as an aid to his or her teaching.

CATP

Caffeine Access Transport Protocol. Common method of moving caffeine across Wide Area Networks such as the *Internet.* CATP was first used at the Binary Cafe in Cybertown and quickly spread worldwide. There are reported problems with short-circuits and rust and decaffeinated beverages were not supported until version 1.5.3

CAV

Constant Angular Velocity playback in magnetic and laser discs where the disc rotates at a constant speed. Relative to CLV variable speeds, the CAV approach results in varying data retrieval times that depend upon where the read/write head is located relative to the disc spindle. Authors of CAV disc products try to locate commonly accessed files closer to spindle. In videodiscs, CAV discs hold only 30 minutes of video on each side of a 12-inch disc. However, CAV facilitates searching for individual frames. See also **CLV**.

cc

abbreviation for Carbon Copy. To cc: an e-mail message to someone is to send him or her a copy of the e-mail message.

CD

a 'small' injection-moulded optical disc containing digitised information that has been recorded with a laser device and must be read on a laser device. The term 'small' generally refers to a disc that is 8 cm or 12 cm (4.72 inches) in diameter as opposed to videodiscs that typically are much larger in diameter. Also, videodiscs usually are restricted to analog inputs from videotape whereas CDs rely on inputs from computer tape or other digitised platforms. Although there are several types of CDs for audio, television and computer playback, the CD-Audio and CD-ROM discs have overwhelming shares of the market. For example, an expert has discussed why CD-ROM discs are replacing floppy discs in a 'ground swell'. CD-ROM discs now hold approximately 680 Mb (i.e., 680 million characters) although compression techniques make it possible to record CDs from even larger computer files. Usually CDs have slower access speeds than magnetic hard drives, but speeds are improving and playback of video is now possible on both CD-ROM and CD-I players. Although the best-known CDs once were those that contain only audio recordings, there is a rapidly growing market for various types of CDs that contain computer files and/or files that can be read on special devices connected to television sets.

CD recording

see **CD-R** and **CD-DVD.**

CD+g

audio CD plus still-image graphics such as with Photo CD. Although these are commonly displayed on television screens, they are less interactive than CD-I, CD-VIS, CD-R, CD-Karaoke, CD-3DO, CD-MM and CD-TV. See also **CD-Karaoke.**

CD32

the 32-bit multimedia CD system that plays on Amiga Computers from Commodore Corporation. These CDs are used for CD movies, games and educational material on Amiga Computers. The future of the CD32 is clouded by the 1994 declaration of bankruptcy by Commodore Corporation. See also **Amiga**.

CD-3Do

a type of compact disc designed originally to compete against CD-I and CD-MM for interactive television set entertainment and, possibly, education. A promoter named Trip Hawkins put together an impressive grouping of Hollywood movie studios and other developers of interactive videos using MPEG compression. Large companies are producing playback machines for TV sets. The 3DO video games lost out completely to competitors who agreed upon a competing CD-Karaoke standard. Prospects once seemed high that this would emerge a winner. In 1993, 3DO stock soared in price. However, in 1994, sales of 3DO players have fallen far short of expectations (except in Japan) and the 3DO stock price fell from a high of over $45 per share to less than $15. Hawkins invested millions more of his own money in the company. This maker of multimedia game players is fighting for survival. Hawkins and his 3DO machines all but disappeared from the public. However, in May of 1998, they resurfaced 3DO, unveiled 11 video games and targets to become a small and more focussed video game maker.

CD-audio

a CD that contains only audio playback.

CDBUS

see **bus topology.**

CD-DVD

digital Video (or Versatile) Disc combines the best features of CD-ROM size and data storage with capacity for video storage beyond that of videodiscs. DVD is so revolutionary that in the next decade it will probably replace VHS videotapes and CD-ROMs and videodiscs.

A concise review of the current and forthcoming state of the art for home/office recording of DVD discs appears in a famous magazine. Unfortunately, the major vendors are divided between the DVD-RAM Type 1 and 2 standards versus the DVD+RW standard. At present the competition is somewhat hostile, including lawsuits over the use of the DVD logo. DVD-RAM is first on the market, but it is too soon for most of us to abandon our CD-R recorders for DVD-RAM. Although DVD-RAM and DVD+RW discs will read on most DVD players on computers, neither type will play on set-top DVD-Video players for television sets.

■ CD-eraseable

an alternate term for CD-RW compact discs that can be erased and written over with new and/or updated computer files. The key feature of CD-RW is that these CDs will play on newer CD-ROM drives. In 1997, however, virtually all vendors of CD recording hardware offer a CD-RW drive that will play and record discs that will play on CD-ROM drives. This technology brings the world of CDs closer to the world of videotapes and floppy discs. However, unlike floppy discs holding 1.44 Mb of data, the CDs will hold 650 Mb of data. This makes the recording and revision of multimedia files in a cheap storage medium (possibly less than one dollar) a feasible option. See **CD-DVD.**

■ CDF

see **RDF**.

■ CD-I

Compact Disc-Interactive.

■ CD-karaoke

the video CD format that were agreed upon and eventually became the standard Video CD format agreed upon by major vendors. Initially, vendors were trying to develop CDs for television sets that each had a different standard analogous to having different track gauges for different railroads. The agreed upon video standard in 1993 at last makes it possible to cross platforms in CDs for television.

■ CDMA/TDMA

Code Division Multiple Access and Time Division Multiple Access. Dual-mode cellular telephones that aid in the receiving of fax and computer network data on computers and PDAs.

■ CD-MM

older CDs that compete with CD-VIS, CD-I and CD-3DO discs that also play back visual as well has audio entertainment and learning materials in a hypermedia format on a television set. These will be replaced with newer players for CD-DVD. CD-MM discs required special players that connected to a television much like a VCR machine. They compete with CD-I discs but are not the same size and will not play on CD-I players. Only discs developed by Sony Corporation will run on CD-MM players. Various CD-MM games, encyclopaedias, hypermedia art books and other consumer products are available on CD-I discs in department stores and video stores. Whereas CD-I and CD-ROM discs may be recorded on CD-R blanks in home recording devices, it is less likely that CD-

MM discs will ever be produced outside professional studios. Users will thus be limited by what company develops and promotes. In 1993, the company agreed to a new CD-format that is more in line with other players in the market. With the initial market shock of CD-3DO, the future of CD-I and CD-MM is seriously in doubt. See also **CD-DVD, CD-3DO, CD-Karaoke, CD-VIS** and **CD-I.**

■ CDPD

Cellular Digital Packet Data. Technology that facilitates more traffic on existing cellular networks. CDPD hardware is required for sending e-mail to PDAs.

■ CD-R or CD-RW

a term used for machines (drives) that will record CD laser discs that will read on standard CD-ROM drives. CD 'encoding' depicts the recording (burning or transfer of files) to a CD, whereas CD 'decoding' depicts the reading of those files. The term CD-Erasable in the early 1990s depicted recording of erasable CDs that could not be read only in special drives rather than CD-ROM drives. In times past, CD-R depicted a recordable CD blank disc also known as a CD-WORM disc. CD-R is now an obsolete term since, in 1997, CD-RW discs also known as CD-RW or CD-Rewritable discs made 'read only memory' a thing of the past. Of course it is always possible to file protect and computer files in any type of storage so that they cannot be overwritten. In 1997, virtually all the manufacturers of CD-RW recording machines for CD-ROMs will offer CD-Erasable drives that will likely replace most CD-R technology up to 1997. Laser recording machines typically connect to a computer's SCSI or IDE controller. High-end desktop computers now come with CD-R or CD-RW recorders and players all in the same drive. Costs of a CD-R recorder have fallen by over 90% to less than $800. Recording CDs of any type is often referred to as 'burning' or 'baking'. A CD recorder will not record every type of CD. Virtually all of them record CD-ROM discs and some will record CD-I discs. Rewritable versions are also available, but these will not play back on standard CD-ROM drives. CD-DVD recording requires more expensive hardware. Some record CD-Karaoke with appropriate software. Some CDs such as CD-MM and CD-3DO cannot usually be recorded on home recorders. CD-ROM and other types of CDs can be reproduced for less than $1 per disc.

CD-R2

see **CD-DVD.**

CD-ROM

Compact Disc-Read Only Memory. This is now an obsolete term since, in 1997, CD-RW discs also known as CD-Rewritable discs made 'read only memory' a thing of the past. These 5.25 inch discs can be recorded, written over at will (unless file protected) and played back from computers connected to proper recording and/or playback drives. The CD-RW drives become like hard drives or floppy disc drives in that CD-RW discs may store files that can be executed in software packages such as word processors, spreadsheet software, ToolBook books and HyperCard stacks. Some users want them to serve as auxiliary storage devices for computer text, audio and video files. CD-RW drives will eventually be replaced by CD-DVD drives for DVD and DVD-RAM discs that are the same size but hold more than 20 times as much data. The problem for DVD is that CD-ROM drives exist in millions of computers and it will take time for the newer DVD hardware to take over as a standard. Presently, it is also much cheaper to record (encode) CD-RW discs using CD-R recorders. See also **CD-DVD** and **CD-ROM titles.**

CD-ROM titles

books and games available on CD-ROM discs. Comparisons are difficult, because there are thousands in hundreds of markets.

CD-ROM XA

see **CD-ROM.**

CD-RW

see **CD-ROM.**

CDSL

Consumer Digital Subscriber Line. Rockwell's new technology for digital modems that will use regular telephone lines and run at speeds up to 1 MBps. See **ADSL** and **DSL.**

CD-stand alone

reference to audio/video players that stand alone in the sense of not needing a computer. The term generally refers to set-top video boxes for network television or to CD players such as CD-3DO, CD-I, CD-MM, CD-TV, CD-VIS, etc. See also **Set-top box** and **CD**

CD-TV

Commodore Dynamic-Total Vision player manufactured by Commodore Corporation to compete with CD-I, CD-MM, CD-VIS and CD-3DO CD players for television sets. CD-TV discs are viewed in television sets from a CD-TV player or on Amiga video computers. They may not, however, be played on CD-ROM players. The market share of CD-TV is so small that its future is quite uncertain and is clouded by the 1994 declaration of bankruptcy by Commodore Corporation. See also **CD-I, CD-3DO, CD-MM, CD-VIS, Games.**

CD-VIS

the Memorex MD-2500 Visual Information System CD player marketed by a company that competes with CD-MM, CD-I and CD-3DO discs that also play back visual as well has audio interactive entertainment on television sets. The Memorex MD-2500 requires no host computer to perform interactive operations from a remote control. Compton's Multimedia Encyclopaedia disc and some other discs are available, but the market share of CD-VIS never became great enough to attract widespread authorship of VIS discs. At present there are very few titles and interest in CD-VIS relative to CD-I and CD-3DO is waning.

CD-WORM

see **CD-R.**

censorship

issues frequently arise online about censorship. When does a service provider or a mail discussion list host or a message base host have a right to delete material others have posted? When posts are clearly illegal, such as posting a copyrighted work of text or media without permission from the copyright holder, they must be deleted as soon as they are recognised. The host or provider may become liable if they don't take action. But what about the online Forum host who deletes a political post that he or she disagrees with? Is this censorship? Are there First Amendment rights to protect such posts? Deleting a disagreeable, but legal post is certainly a form of censorship. But it has nothing to do with First Amendment rights. The First Amendment applies to governments and their agents, not to individuals. The Forum host who deletes material does so at his or her own risk. The risk is not a legal one, but whether such a deletion meets the needs of the community that the host represents. The online host may gain or lose membership from the community, if the community at large agrees or disagrees with the action. Censorship in such cases is more a moral and social issue than a legal one.

Central Processing Unit (CPU)

the main silicon chip that runs a computer's operating system and application software. It performs a computer's essential mathematical functions and controls essential operations. Intel CPUs in PCs were numbered by generation: 286, 386, 486. This numbering scheme was abandoned by Intel with the Pentium CPU, which would be the 586 and the Pentium Pro, which would the 686. Motorola PowerPC CPUs have maintained a consistent numbering convention: 601, 603, 604.

CERN

the European Organisation for Nuclear Research where the web was born. The original name in French was Conseil Européen pour la Recherche Nucléaire (CERN).

■ certificate, public key

specially formatted block of data that contains a public key and the name of its owner. The certificate carries the digital signature of a certification authority to authenticate it.

■ CFML

Cold Fusion Markup Language for creation of dynamic and interactive Web pages. Along with the usual Hypertext Markup Language (HTML) tags that determine page layout and appearance, the page creator uses CFML tags to bring in content based on the results of a database query or user input. CMFL is a proprietary language developed for use with Cold Fusion.

■ CGI

Common Gateway Interface is one of the most popular UNIX-based programs/devices that supply interfaces between browsers and servers on the Internet. A standard for running external programs from a World-Wide Web HTTP server. CGI specifies how to pass dynamic components to the executing program as part of the HTTP request. For example, it will allow answers typed into an HTML form on the client computer to be tabulated and stored in a database on the server-side computer. Commonly, the server-side CGI program will generate some HTML, which will be passed back to the client's browser. For example, it might report to the client user that the form is not filled out properly or report the invoice total of an order. CGI allows the returned HTML (or other document type) to depend in any arbitrary way on the request. The CGI program can, for example, access information in a database and format the results as HTML. CGI is not a programming language. There are various 'CGI' scripting programs. Perl is a common choice for writing CGI scripts in UNIX code. Some HTTP servers require CGI programs to reside in a special directory, often '/cgi-bin' but better servers provide ways to distinguish CGI programs so they can be kept in the same directories as the HTML files to which they are related. In order to improve performance, Netscape devised NSAPI and Microsoft developed the ISAPI standard, which allow CGI-like tasks to run as part of the host server process, thus avoiding the overhead of creating a new process to handle each CGI invocation.

■ CGI-bin

the most common name of a directory on a web server in which CGI programs are stored.

■ chain letter

a form of spam which asks you to distribute the letter to many other people. They are against the policies of most Internet service providers and almost always are hoaxes. Many of them promise quick ways to make money, usually on the basis of pyramid schemes, which are illegal.

■ channel

transmission line that can carry the sound of a separate MIDI instrument. Each MIDI port allows up to 16 separate channels for sending or receiving data. Each channel can function as a separate instrument in an ensemble, each using its own patch and responding independently to continuous controllers.

Channel has another meaning on the World Wide Web.

■ charset

short for character set. Different character sets are used for different purposes such as the different characters used by different languages.

■ chat

a form of interactive online communication that enables typed conversations to occur in real-time. When participating in a chat discussion, your messages are instantaneously relayed to other members in the chat room while other members' messages are instantaneously relayed to you.

■ chat history

a transcript of a chat session.

■ chat lines or chat rooms

real time Internet conversations (written or oral) that transpire in real (synchronous) time as opposed to conferencing (e.g., message board posting and topic classification. There are many sources for free chat software downloads.

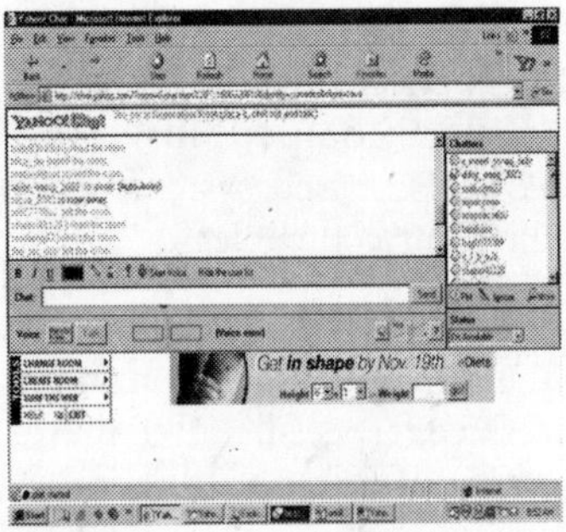

■ chatter's block

a condition characterised by excessive anxiety about sending chat messages. The chatter with chatter's block feels that every message he types in a chat must be perfectly worded and perfectly timed. By striving to meet these standards of perfection, the chatter constantly erases and rewords his messages, often deciding not to send the messages at all. The cure for chatter's block is to relax. Everyone in a chat is expressing (and typing) ideas quickly and no one will blink an eye at the odd typo.

■ checksum

a mathematical calculation applied to the contents of a packet before and after it is sent. If the 'before' calculation does not match the 'after' calculation, there were errors in the transmission.

CHRP

Common Hardware Reference Platform. Architecture in processors for Power PCs. This term has been replaced by 'PowerPC Reference Platform' and is IBM's open system standard intended to ensure compatibility among PowerPC-based systems built by different companies.

churn

the turnover of users on an online service, especially after the expiration of a free trial period.

CIDR

Classless Inter-Domain Routing. This is a change in specifying ranges of IP addresses from the old Class A, B and C address blocks. IP addresses consist of 32 bits, usually expressed in four 8-bit numbers, such as 122.63.101.17. In the old system, Class C specified 24 bits (the first three numbers in the conventional IP address), leaving all the addresses in the remaining 8 bits to be assigned by the registrant (256 addresses, less a few broadcast only addresses). Class B specified 16 bits and class A, 8 bits, leaving the balance to the registrant. Now, the IP address is followed by an IP Prefix, such as 122.63.101.14/26. The /26 IP Prefix means that the first 26 bits of the given IP address are fixed and the registrant has the remaining 6 bits (64 addresses) to use and assign. IP Prefixes are currently used ranging from /27 (2^5 or 32 addresses) to /13 (2^{19} or 524,288 addresses.

cipher

procedure that transforms data between plaintext and ciphertext, a crypto algorithm.

Cipher Block Chaining (CBC)

block cipher mode that combines the previous block of ciphertext with the current block of plaintext before encrypting it. Very widely used.

Cipher Feedback (CFB)

block cipher mode that feeds previously encrypted ciphertext through the block cipher to generate the key that encrypts the next block of ciphertext. Also called CTAK.

ciphertext

data that has been encrypted with a cipher, as opposed to plaintext.

Ciphertext Autokey (CTAK)

block cipher mode that feeds previously encrypted ciphertext through the block cipher to generate the key that encrypts the next block of ciphertext. Also called CFB.

CISC

Complex Instruction Set Computing. Chipsets such as the Intel family of popular 386, 486 and Pentium competitors and the Motorola 680x0 family in Mac computers. These were the most popular processors until the RISC alternatives entered the market. The future of CISC versus RISC is now up in the air.

See also **Pentium, USENet** and **RISC.**

■ CLEC

Competitive Local Exchange Carrier. See **LEC**.

■ click through

the process of clicking on a link in a search engine output page to visit an indexed site. This is an important link in the process of receiving visitors to a site via search engines. Good ranking may be useless if visitors do not click on the link, which leads to the indexed site. The secret here is to provide a good descriptive title and an accurate and interesting description.

■ client

a software program that is used to contact and obtain data from a *Server* software program on another computer, often across a great distance. Each client program is designed to work with one or more specific kinds of Server programs and each *Server* requires a specific kind of Client. A Web browser is a specific kind of client.

■ client-server architecture

in client-server architecture, the computing load is distributed among the many clients (individual computers) in a network, drawing information from central servers of the information. On the Internet, a web browser is a client that runs software locally that processes information received from central servers of the information. The opposite of client server architecture is the situation where a central powerful computer does all the processing, feeding the results to dumb terminals which do little more than communicate requests and feed back the results processed centrally.

■ clipboard

a holding device that contains the most recently copied or cut text or image such that contents of the clipboard can be pasted one or more times into other parts of the document at hand or other documents. It is usually possible to cross between different software options such as between Windows programs.

■ clipper

integrated circuit containing crypto functions for voice and telephone using the SKIPJACK cipher and the Escrowed Encryption Standard. It failed to find a customer base and is no longer manufactured.

■ clipper chip

the Clipper Chip is a cryptographic device being promoted by the U.S. government. Its purported advantage is that it provides a standard for securing private voice communication. With Clipper, however, the government has the opportunity to obtain decryption keys that are held in escrow by two government agencies. Although the Clipper proposal requires legal authorisation to obtain these keys, the history of illegal domestic surveillance by Federal agencies makes the existence of this 'back-door' decryption channel a cause for concern.

■ cloaking

the hiding of page content. Normally carried out to stop page thieves stealing optimised pages.

■ clock speed

the speed of the processor is measured with the clock frequency. The processor consistently works internally at the same clock frequency. The IBM PC has a clock frequency of 4.77 MHz (Megahertz). Compatibles sometimes use higher frequencies, but higher speeds may create compatibility problems.

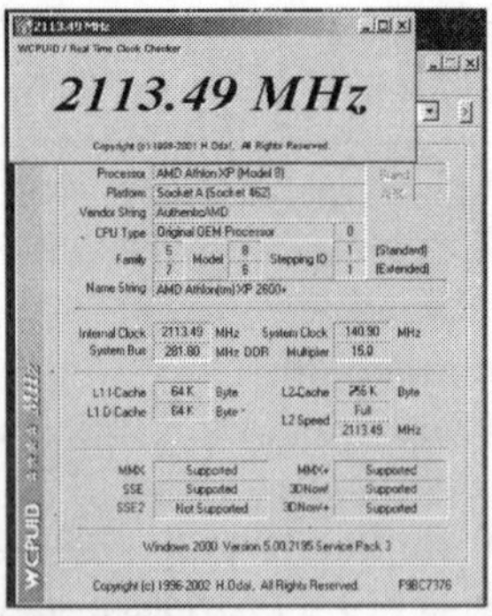

■ clustering

the listing of only one page from each web site in a search engine or directory's list of search results. This avoids occupation of all the top results by a small number of web sites and makes the list of results clearer and more useful to the user.

■ CLV

Constant Linear Velocity. Playback in magnetic and laser discs where the disc rotates at varying speeds. Relative to CAV constant speeds, the CAV approach results in constant data retrieval times that do not depend upon where the read/write head is located relative to the disc spindle. CLV videodiscs hold up to 60 minutes of video per side of a 12-inch disc. However, CLV discs cannot be searched for individual frames as effectively as CAV discs. See also **CAV.**

■ CMC

Computer Mediated Communication, a very broad term that encompasses chat lines, virtual communities and other forms of communication.

■ coaxial cable

a cable consisting of a single metal wire surrounded by insulation, which is itself surrounded by a braided or foil outer conductor.

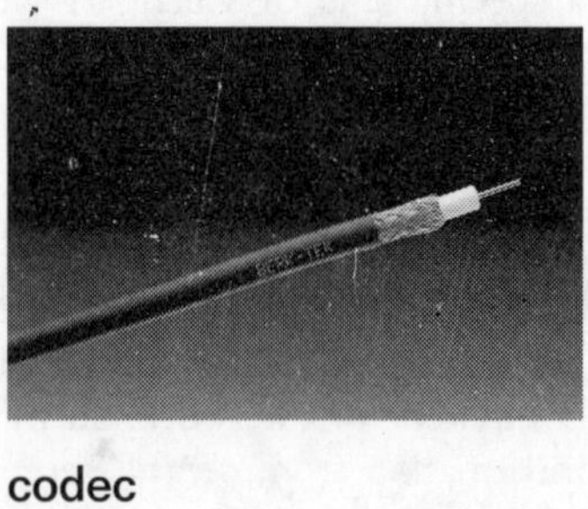

■ codec

hardware and software for compressing and decompressing large volumes of data. The term generally applies to large multimedia files.

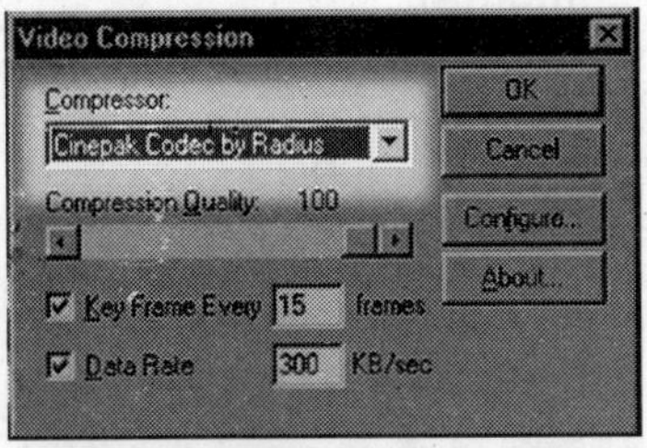

■ **collaboration**

a joint effort that network technology has facilitated with email, FTP and more advanced means of sharing ideas, documents and data. Writing has become more of a collaborative effort since the dawn of the WWW. The WWW takes authors beyond the telephone by enabling them to speak to one another (audio), see one another (videoconferencing) and visualise documents and data. See also **CMC, IRC, videoconferencing, groupware** and **virtual.**

■ **collar**

a derivative instruments investing term where an investor puts a 'collar' around investment risk, usually by selling a put option (an option to purchase) and purchasing a call option (an option to sell) around an investment. Two famous companies sold put warrants on their own common stock and then used the proceeds to purchase calls on the same stock. This process is called a 'costless collar' and is used to express a bullish view of the stock by management.

■ **collision detection**

the process by which a node on a network monitors the communications line to determine when a collision (two nodes attempting to transmit at the same time) has occurred.

■ **co-location**

most often used to refer to having a server that belongs to one person or group physically located on an Internet-connected network that belongs to another person or group. Usually this is done because the server owner wants their machine to be on a high-speed Internet connection and/or they do not want the security risks of having the server on their own network.

■ **comment**

the HTML <!— and —> tags are used to hide text from browsers. Some search engines ignore text between these symbols but others index such text as if the comment tags were not there. Comments are often used to hide JavaScript code from non-compliant browsers and sometimes to provide invisible keywords to some search engines.

■ **commercial online service**

a computer network that supplies its members with access to chat rooms, bulletin boards and other online content on a monthly fee basis. Commercial online services include America Online, CompuServe, The Microsoft Network and Prodigy. In addition to their own proprietary content, most commercial online services also provide access to the Internet.

■ Common Gateway Interface (CGI)

a standard used by programmers that allows their programs to interact with the World Wide Web. CGI scripts can be written in many computer languages, but Perl and C are the most common.

■ compile

to have a computer translate code written in a computer language into an executable form.

■ compression

a technology that reduces the size of a file. Compression programs like WinZip and UNIX compress are valuable to network users because they help save both time and bandwidth.

■ Compuserve

a commercial network that has some of the 'richest offerings available, but it has been the slowest to change and can be much costlier than the other two services, especially if you make heavy use of some of its best features' according to a survey. It has a wide choice of bulletin boards, U.S. news and world reports magazine and Navigator to the Internet. News services are relatively cheap, but modem line costs are somewhat expensive. See also **networks, Internet, SLIP, America Online** and **eWorld.**

■ computer

an electronic system that can store and process information under program control.

■ Computer Emergency Response Team (CERT)

organisation that collects and distributes information on computer security incidents and software problems relating to publicly used networks like the Internet.

■ Computer Incident Advisory Capability (CIAC)

organisation established by the Department of Energy to track and report on computer security relevant events and situations.

■ computer literacy

knowledge about and the ability to learn about computers.

■ computer virus

see **virus**.

■ confidentiality

the ability to ensure that information is not disclosed to people who aren't explicitly intended to receive it.

■ configuration

this is a general-purpose computer term that can refer to the way you have your computer set up. It is also used to describe the total combination of hardware components that make up a computer system and the software settings that allow various hardware components of a computer system to communicate with one another.

■ configure

the act of changing software or hardware actions by changing the settings.

■ congestion

a state occurring in a part of a network when the message traffic is so heavy that it slows down network response time.

■ connection

when two computers have established a path through which the exchange of information can occur.

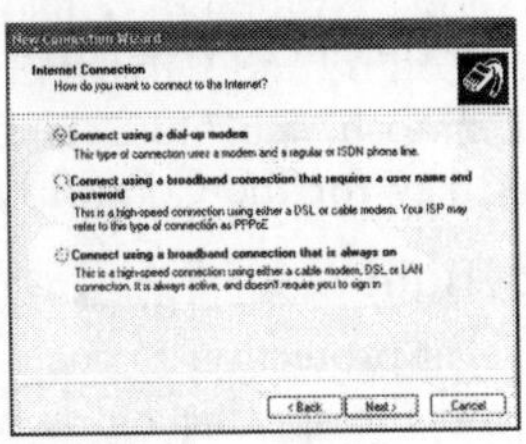

■ console

the file server.

■ Consulting Committee, International Telephone and Telegraph (CCITT)

international standards committee for telephone communications systems.

■ content

generally, the information provided on a web page, as opposed to its design and layout. Content can take the form of text, graphics, audio, video or a searchable database.

■ control code

special nonprinting codes that cause electronic equipment to perform specific actions.

■ cookie

the most common meaning of 'Cookie' on the Internet refers to a piece of information sent by a Web Server to a Web Browser that the Browser software is expected to save and to send back to the Server whenever the browser makes additional requests from the Server. Depending on the type of Cookie used and the Browsers' settings, the Browser may accept or not accept the Cookie and may save the Cookie for either a short time or a long time. Cookies might contain information such as login or registration information, online 'shopping cart' information, user preferences, etc. When a Server receives a request from a Browser that includes a Cookie, the Server is able to use the information stored in the Cookie. For example, the Server might customise what is sent back to the user or keep a log of particular users' requests. Cookies are usually set to expire after a predetermined amount of time and are usually saved in memory until the

Browser software is closed down, at which time they may be saved to disk if their 'expire time' has not been reached. Cookies do not read your hard drive and send your life story to the CIA, but they can be used to gather more information about a user than would be possible without them.

■ coopetition

the phenomena of computer companies cooperating with their competitors on a project-by-project basis.

■ coprocessor

electronic component that relieves the microprocessor of some important tasks. Increased performance can often be achieved through the use of coprocessors. For example, a math coprocessor performs many of the math operations outside the microprocessor. A coprocessor may also speed graphics computations.

■ copy protection

a software lock placed on a computer program by its developer to thwart piracy. This preventative measure was widely used in the mid-1980s but later abandoned by many developers because of numerous customer complaints.

■ copy-and-paste, cut-and-paste

the technique of copying text from one location or file to another. If the text in the original location is deleted, it is called cut-and-paste. Whether cutting or copying, the process begins by positioning the cursor at one end of the text to be copied and clicking and dragging to the other end to highlight the text. Or if you want to copy the entire text on a page, use Edit/Select All or press Control and the letter A simultaneously.

At this point, there are three common ways to cut or copy and then paste. Which ones work may vary by the software you are using.

Select Edit and then Copy or Cut from the pull-down menus in your software. Then position your cursor in the location you want to copy to, even if it is in a different window and then select Edit and Paste.

Right click on the highlighted text and select Cut or Copy. Position the cursor in the location to be copied to and right click and select Paste.

Press the Control key and the X key together to cut or Control and C to copy. Position the cursor and press Control and V to paste. With a Macintosh, substitute the Command key for the Control key.

■ copyright

the legal protection against copying and the specific rights allowing copying given to original works, which may be in printed or photographically or electronically stored words, music, visual arts and performing arts. The purpose of copyright is not just to protect the rights, but to establish the rules under which copies or portions may be made to make a work more widely available. Copyright extends to electronic representations of these forms, too, although the laws governing new electronic copies in such forms as search engine indexes and browser caches needs better definition. Copyright exists on all original works from the moment they are published, whether formally registered or not and whether or not copyright markings appear on the works. Copyrights probably apply to public postings in e-mail, message bases and newsgroups, but the law is not well tested in these areas. Copyrights are observed by most countries in the world.

■ CORBA

Common Object Request Broker Architecture. It is in competition with Microsoft's OLE/DCOM object-oriented Middleware technology for business applications. CORBA is most popular in communications Middleware using an Object Request Broker ORB. CORBA evolved out of TCP/IP. DCOM is bundled with the Windows 2000 operating system but has lacklustre support for other operating systems. CORBA is more flexible with other operating systems. Both CORBA and OLE/DCOM are designed to distribute objects or assembly of appplications from discreet, self-contained components. Both are appealing in the fast growing technology of 'object middleware'. Object middleware has corporate appeal due to the ability to provide highly abstracted object-oriented programming interfaces. Microsoft added new terminology in this area. For example, COM depicts a Component Object Model to describe the base model used for building components. The term DCOM is the Distributed form of COM. ActiveX (formerly OCX) is the packaging technology for controls and supercedes prior Visual Basic Controls known as VBX. OLE no longer means object linking and embedding. OLE now refers to a collection of technologies. XML is a technology for conveying structured data in a portable way. CORBA allows users to connect disparate systems and form object architectures. XML will allow users to transmit structured information within, between and out of those systems and to represent information in a universal way in and across architectures. Both technologies are platform, vendor and language independent. The conceptual fit is perfect.

■ country code

most countries in the world that are connected to the Internet have been assigned two-letter country codes by the international standard ISO 3166. These two letter codes are the major domain addresses for the country.

■ CPU

Central Processing Unit that encompasses a computer's RAM,

processing and control circuitry, including the arithmetic-logic (ALU) unit. Both the ALU and the control units are wholly contained on the microprocessing chip whereas the primary storage is on the motherboard or the expansion bus.

■ **cracker**

a malicious hacker who breaks (or cracks) the security of computer systems in order to access, steal or destroy sensitive information. 'Hacker' is often incorrectly used instead of cracker, especially by the media. Crackers try to exploit weaknesses in system security or in some cases, the weaknesses of its users who can be tricked into revealing passwords.

■ **cracking**

the process of overcoming a security measure. Cracking a key means an attempt to recover the key's value, cracking some ciphertext means an attempt to recover the corresponding plaintext.

■ **cram, cramming**

cramming is the practice by some phone companies, yours or others, to add false charges to your phone bills for calls you never made.

■ **crawler**

see **spider**.

■ **CRC**

acronym for Cyclic Redundancy Check. A technique of providing a data string added to packets of information that can be used to detect errors in the data packets. In the OSI or TCP/IP network models, CRC is added to a packet frame at the Data Link Layer.

■ **critical application**

computing application where an attacker could cause incredibly serious damage, including loss of life.

■ **CRM**

Customer Relationship Management. System based upon information technology. Central to CRM are databases customer relationships in sufficient detail so that management, salespeople, people providing service and perhaps the customer directly could access information, match customer needs with product plans and offerings, remind customers of service requirements, know what other products a customer had purchased and so forth.

■ **crossload**

to send an attached file via e-mail.

■ **cross-posting**

to post a single message simultaneously to multiple news-groups or discussion groups. Gratuitous cross posting is considered poor Netiquette.

■ **crunch**

to efficiently process large amounts of information. A number cruncher, for example, is a routine or device optimised for and dedicated to processing numbers.

■ **cryptanalysis**

process of trying to recover crypto keys or plaintext associated with a crypto system.

■ **cryptography, crypto**

mechanisms to protect information by applying transformations to it that are hard to reverse without some secret knowledge.

■ **cryptolope**

the combination of 'cryptographic' security encryption with 'envelopes' of domain. Cryptolopes enable publishers on the WWW to securely distribute content with copyright protections and security over payments for copyrighted material usage.

■ **cryptoperiod**

amount of time a particular key is used, some times refers to the amount of data encrypted with it.

■ **CSS**

Cascading Style Sheet. A standard for specifying the appearance of text and other elements. CSS was developed for use with *HTML* in Web pages but is also used in other situations, notably in applications built using *XPFE*. CSS is typically used to provide a single 'library' of styles that are used over and over throughout a large number of related documents, as in a web site. A CSS file might specify that all numbered lists are to appear in *italics*. By changing that single specification the look of a large number of documents can be easily changed.

■ **CWIS**

Campus Wide Information System bulletin board services that can be accessed on the Internet. These are available on most college campuses and provide bulletin board information on campus calendars, e-mail directories on the campus, employment opportunities, campus events, course catalogues, etc.

■ **cybermall**

a term commonly used to describe an electronic site shared by a number of commercial interests.

■ **cyberspace**

1. the place where computer networking hardware, network software and people using them converge.
2. the prefix 'cyber' is often combined with other words, as in 'cyberpunk'.

■ **cybersquatting**

the act of registering a company name as a domain name by someone outside the company in hopes of selling it to the company for a profit. Anti-cybersquatting legislation has been introduced to make it illegal.

■ DAB/DAR

'Digital Audio Broadcast' and 'Digital Audio Radio' broadcasting in digital formats via satellites and fibre optic cable.

■ DAC

'Digital Analog Conversion' hardware that converts digital signals into analog form.

■ daemon

in the UNIX operating system, a background process that lies dormant waiting to perform some useful task. The sendmail daemon, for example, continually runs but becomes active only when e-mail is sent or received.

■ DAT

Digital Audio Tape. It is used for recording computer disc files onto a cheap backup and storage medium. DAT tapes are contained in small cartridges that are the cheapest means of storing vast amounts of data. For example, a cartridge smaller than the palm of an adult hand can hold two or more gigabyes of data.

■ data encryption key

a string of characters used to mathematically encode a message so that it can only be read by someone in possession of another related key.

■ Data Encryption Standard (DAS)

the Data Encryption Standard or DES, was the first official U.S. government cipher intended for commercial use. DES is the most widely used cryptosystem in the world.

■ data link

the portion of a system of computers that transfers data between them, including wiring, hardware, interfaces and device driver software.

■ database

a collection of data records. On web databases, records may consist of web pages or graphics or audio files or newspaper files or books or movies or press releases or almost anything from very general to very specific areas of interest. Records may or may not be further broken into fields. Database records are usually indexed and come with a search interface to find records of interest.

■ datagram

in TCP/IP networks, datagram is a synonym for packet.

■ DAV

Digital Audio Video. Connectors such as those found on the Apple

AV that allow the flow of digitised video to bypass the computer's main bus.

■ db2

see **database**.

■ dbx

the 'companding' compression and expansion of audio signals to reduce noise distortions of stereo television broadcasts. See also **MTS/SAP**.

■ DCC

Digital Compact Cassette. Format that improves sound quality relative to traditional analog formats of audio cassettes. Analog cassettes can be played on DCC tape decks such that the purchase of a DCC tape deck does not preclude listening to analog tapes.

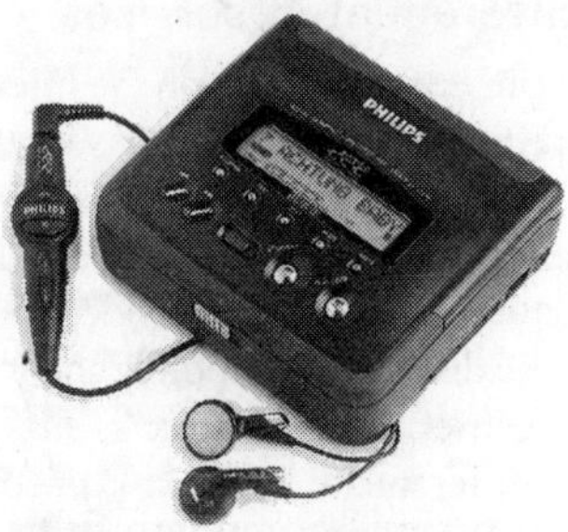

■ DCOM

see **CORBA**.

■ dead link

an Internet link which doesn't lead to a page or site, probably because the server is down or the page has moved or no longer exists. Most search engines have techniques for removing such pages from their listings automatically, but as the Internet continues to increase in size, it becomes more and more difficult for a search engine to check all the pages in the index regularly. Reporting of dead links helps to keep the indexes clean and accurate and this can usually be done by submitting the dead link to the search engine.

■ debugging

executing a program, one statement at a time, to identify and fix errors.

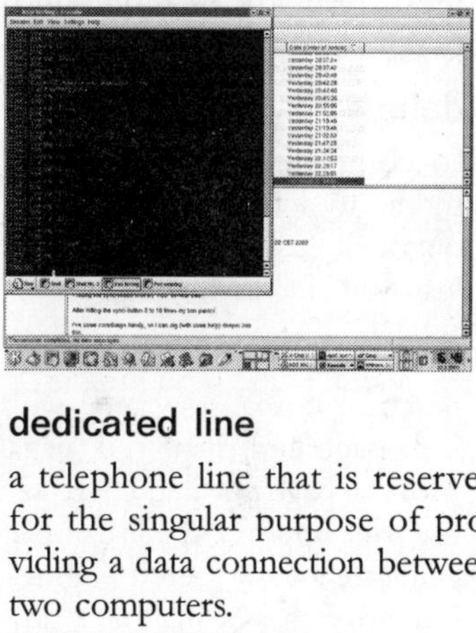

■ dedicated line

a telephone line that is reserved for the singular purpose of providing a data connection between two computers.

■ de-listing

the removal of pages from a search engine's index. Removal can occur for various reasons, including unreliability of the machine that hosts a site or because of perceived attempts at spamdexing.

■ delivery receipt

an optional e-mail feature that notifies you when your e-mail message has been delivered to its recipient.

Delphi

1. Delphi Forums. An Internet service and content provider. It was established in 1983 and was the first national provider to add Internet access in 1992.
2. an application development language from Inprise (formerly Borland).
3. a method of forecasting future developments based on repeated surveys of experts with anonymous feedback of results in between rounds of questioning.

delurk

to come out of online lurking mode, to actively participate in a online discussion after a period of just watching or lurking.

description

descriptive text associated with a web page and displayed, usually with the page title and URL, when the page appears in a list of pages generated by a search engine or directory as a result of a query. Some search engines take this description from the Description Meta tag - others generate their own from the text in the page. Directories often use text provided at registration.

device driver

software component that controls a peripheral device. For data link devices, it manages the process of sending and receiving data across the data link.

device driver interface

standard interface used by a host's software to communicate with peripheral devices, including data link devices.

DHTML

Dynamic Hypertext Markup Language. DHTML refers to Web pages that use a combination of HTML, JavaScript and CSS to create features such as letting the user drag items around on the web page, some simple kinds of animation and many more.

dial-up connection

the most popular form of Net connection for the home user, this is a connection from your computer to a host computer over standard telephone lines.

differentiated services

at present, all packets on the Internet are treated alike, regardless of their importance. If you want an important message to be delivered immediately or a streaming video signal to be distributed smoothly and without interruptions, there is no way to differentiate between immediate needs and routine transmissions which could be delayed for a long time without any problems. There are currently efforts under way to test and develop standards for differentiated services, where high priority data can be sent through or around clogged nodes ahead of low priority data. The high priority data transmission will cost more, of course.

■ **Diffie-Hellman (DH)**

public key crypto algorithm that generates a shared secret between two entities after they publicly share some randomly generated data.

■ **digerati**

the digital version of literati, it is a reference to a vague cloud of people seen to be knowledgeable, hip or otherwise in-the-know in regards to the digital revolution.

■ **Digital Nervous System (DNS)**

a term used by Bill Gates in frequent speeches in 1997 and 2000. Gates described a future merging of PCs and communications in a wireless networked environment that made it easy for people to navigate and share information. He spoke of a wireless pocket tablet ('a computer in every pocket') that would enhance communications from many sources, aids in pattern recognition and largely replace telephone calls and paper messages and form in business.

■ **digital signature**

data value generated by a public key algorithm based on the contents of a block of data and a private key, yielding an individualised crypto checksum.

■ **Digital Signature Standard (DSS)**

digital signature algorithm developed by the NSA and endorsed by NIST.

■ **Digital Video (DV) camcorder**

see **video camera** and **video from digital (DV) camcorders.**

■ **DIP switch**

Dual In-line package case on a computer board that contains small switches for configuring hardware components. A given board can be configured in a way that is compatible with the entire system of other peripheral hardware. See also **board.**

■ **direct connection**

a permanent connection between your computer system and the Internet. This is sometimes referred to as a leased-line connection because the line is leased from the telephone company.

■ **direct hit**

a system which monitors the search engine users' selections from search engine results, counting which results are clicked on most and how long visitors spend at that site, so as to improve relevancy. Used by HotBot and as a plug-in to Apple's new innovative Sherlock search system.

■ **directory**

a server or a collection of servers dedicated to indexing Internet web pages and returning lists of pages which match particular queries. Directories (also known as Indexes) are normally compiled manually, by user submission and often involve an editorial selection and/or categorisation process.

■ distributed network computing

distributed network computing where a network computer can perform computing functions in another computer on the same network. In the early days of the Internet, Telnet could be used for remote computing. In modern times, the trend is toward database access and computing among networked computers.

Development tools for data enabled frameworks are starting to emerge. New standards are also starting to emerge like CORBA's IIOP, RMI and Microsoft's DCOM. RMI is part of the Java programming language library, which enables a Java program running on one computer to access the objects and methods of another Java program running on a different computer. Some vendors are also having their own proprietary extensions as well. IIOP is built upon CORBA technology. DCOM is Microsoft Corporation's standard for distributed network computing.

■ dither

to simulate a colour that is not part of the current palette on-screen (or in print) by combining pixels of different colours close to each other. Viewed from a distance, it gives the effect of the colour. Viewed closely, the dots are visible. Dithering can give a noisy appearance to a picture on-screen, but it often can be avoided by selecting non-dithering colours that are compatible with different browsers and platforms. See **RGB**.

■ djvu

pronounced 'deja vu'. It is a compressed graphics format for showing scanned pages on the web. It does for scanned pages what PDF format does for electronically created documents. It requires a plug-in from AT&T. It uses a combination of compression formats that handles sharp-edged text one way and photographs and colour blends another way, thus giving better compression than GIF, JPEG or PNG can do. The server the document is placed on must be set for the MIME types x-djvu, djvu and djv.

■ DLL

Dynamic Link Library. Bundle of coded subroutines that can be shared with different programs on the system.

■ DNS

Domain Name System. A distributed client-server database system which links domain names with their numerical IP addresses.

■ docking station

a platform that can be attached to portable computers giving them a variety of added options such as stereo speakers, a CD-ROM player, an SCSI port and bays for additional components such as data tape drives and floppy disc drives. The numbers and types of options vary among vendors. Some docking stations are small and portable. Others are large and relatively heavy, especially those docking stations that provide notebook computers with added expansion slots for boards such as video capture boards.

■ **document**

when used in reference to the World Wide Web, a document is any file containing text, media or hyperlinks that can be transferred from an HTTP server to a client program.

■ **dogpile**

a meta search engine.

■ **domain**

a sub-set of Internet addresses. Domains are hierarchical and lower-level domains often refer to particular web sites within a top-level domain. The most significant part of the address comes at the end - typical top-level domains are .com, .edu, .gov, .org (which sub-divide addresses into areas of use). There are also various geographic top-level domains (e.g. .ar, .ca, .fr, .ro etc.) referring to particular countries. The relevance to search engine terminology is that web sites, which have their own domain name will often achieve better positioning than web sites which exist as a sub-directory of another organisation's domain.

■ **domainism**

prejudice against people on the basis of their Internet address. For example, adopting a dismissive attitude towards anyone who posts from a commercial online service.

■ **doorway page**

see **Gateway Page.**

■ **DOS**

MS DOS or Microsoft Disk Operating System was introduced by Microsoft Corporation in 1981. It became the operating system standard for PCs around the world and still serves as the foundation of the popular Microsoft Windows extended operating system. The ability to operate from DOS on low-capacity PCs having only 640K of random access memory (RAM) has become the limitation in modern times for DOS to remain a standard for higher speed and higher RAM computers. DOS has not been upgraded for newer 32-bit processors and will eventually fade as the newer 32-bit, 64-bit and higher capacity PCs spread across world markets. See also **Operating system, Windows, Windows Chicago, Windows 2000** and **OS/2.**

■ **dot-com**

nickname for the many commercial businesses that have registered names in the .com domain.

■ **download**

transferring data (usually a file) from another computer to the computer you are using. The opposite of upload.

■ download charges

monetary charges associated with downloading a file from a commercial online service. This method of information exchange is not very popular.

■ DQYDJ

chat slang shorthand for 'Don't quit your day job!'

■ drag

to move an image or a window from one place on the screen to

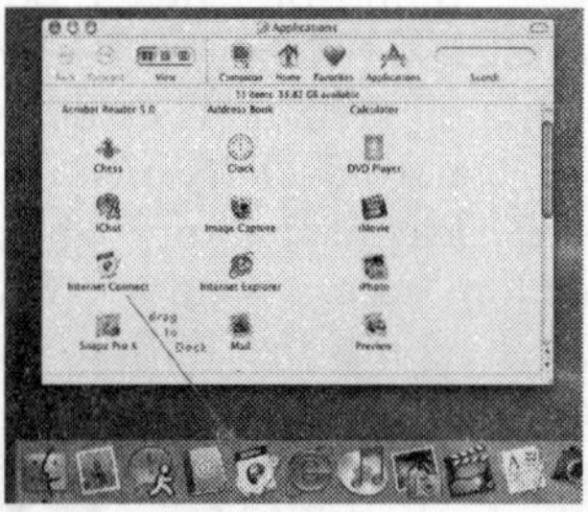

another by grabbing it and pulling it to a new location.

■ driver

a memory resident program usually used to control a hardware device.

■ dry camera

a digital camera that records images directly to a disk or other medium that can be read directly into computers without having to develop imaging film with 'wet' developer chemicals. Various vendors have relatively inexpensive dry cameras whereas these popular vendors have superior and very expensive models that have much higher imaging quality. Some vendors have only the lower priced modes. Photographs can be scanned readers that plug into the back PCs, although the later versions will also plug directly into a PCMCIA slot for downloading into a computer.

■ DSL

Digital Subscriber Line. Technology for transmitting data up to 50 times faster than present analog modem and ISDN alternatives. Telephone companies are hoping that DSL service will keep telephone lines competitive with cable modems and other competitive alternatives to present telephone transmission services. Telephone companies are considering two dominant DSL technologies: Asymmetric Digital Subscriber Line (ADSL, ASL) and High Rate Digital Subscriber Line (HDSL). ADSL technology will deliver higher downstream speeds (6 Mbps) than upstream speeds (640 kbps).

By the way, ADSL or ASL differs from DSL in that there is an asymmetry in transmission speeds into (download) and out of (upload) your computer. In ASL, the upload speeds are much slower than the download speeds. However, ASL connections are being pushed heavily into the huge home market, whereas DSL is being touted for the business firm market.

■ DSP

Digital Signal Processing. Chips that are common in cards (boards) added to expansion slots in computers, especially for adding multimedia to computers. In the future, DSPs and video hardware will probably be more common on motherboards instead of add-on boards. All major sound systems for PCs in the future will probably be upgraded to DSP-based audio chips, many of them right on the motherboard. See also **sound board** and **multimedia video processor**.

■ DSS

Digital Satellite Systems. The term for commercial satellite dishes used for this system is DirectTV, which will compete actively with full-service cable TV. Since 120 channel capacity is expected on small 18-inch home satellite dishes, it becomes much more feasible to bring remote education into homes, schools and offices.

■ DSU

Digital Services Unit. DSU replaces the modem in synchronous connections to the Internet.

■ DTD

Document Type Definition. A document type definition (DTD) that follows the rules of the Standard Generalised Markup Language (SGML). A DTD is a specification that accompanies a document and identifies what the funny little codes (or markup) are that separate paragraphs, identify topic headings and so forth and how each is to be processed. For example, the most common DTD in web documents is HTML. DTD is vital to extracting SGML and XML from web documents and databases that are not marked up with SGML or XML.

■ DTP

DeskTop Publishing or Distributed Transaction Processing. When networking vendors claim 'one billion transactions per day' or quote Transaction Processing Council TPC-C benchmark results, they're talking about DTP. These often-overlooked middleware packages provide the essential communications and other services that enable business logic to be hosted on distributed servers in the middle tier. This business logic is made up of real applications—applications that are vital to most enterprise line-of-business operations. DTP monitors ensure complete transactional integrity for transactions between distributed relational database management systems (RDBMSes). Perhaps more than any other type of middleware, DTP monitors have enabled true three-tier client/server computing.

■ dublin core

a proposed set of standard descriptive metadata elements used with web resources to aid in resource discovery. The elements are intended as a starting point for resource description. The elements are optional and are intended to be extensible to richer descriptive elements when needed. The 15 elements are:

- title
- author/creator
- subject/keywords
- description
- publisher
- other contributor
- date
- resource type
- format resource
- identifier source
- language
- relation
- coverage
- rights management

dump

1. a large mass of information that shows the exact contents of computer memory at a particular time. Dumps are used by programmers in the debugging process.
2. to send a large volume of information to somewhere specific such as a printer or a screen.
3. a backup or a backup file created by the UNIX dump utility.

DVD

see **CD-DVD**.

DVD-RAM

see **CD-DVD.**

DVI

Digital Video Interactive. Video compression hardware and standard developed by the Moving Pictures Experts Group (MPEG) before MPEG video boards hit the market. DVI is a form of compressed full-motion video for computer file storage. Full-motion video at over 30 frames per second takes up so much digitised storage that video must be compressed to make it more useful in hypermedia. DVI was an early compression option that required special and somewhat expensive DVI hardware installation inside the computer of both authors and users (readers) of hypermedia materials. New technology allows for video compression without such expensive hardware. MPEG hardware for video coded compression and decompression seems to be taking over the recent market share lead over DVI largely due to quality of the MPEG and options emerging after DVI. At present, it is not clear whether MPEG or DVI/Indeo will emerge as the international standard with greatest market acceptance. Many analysts are betting on MPEG at the moment.

dynamic content

information on web pages which changes or is changed automatically, e.g. based on database content or user information. Sometimes it's possible to spot that this technique is being used, e.g. if the URL ends with .asp, .cfm, .cgi or

.html. It is possible to serve dynamic content using standard (normally static) .htm or .html type pages, though. Search engines will currently index dynamic content in a similar fashion to static content, although they will not usually index URLs which contain the '?' character.

Dynamic HTML (DHTML)

a more powerful model for HTML that allows absolute control of positioning of elements on a page and more powerful control of events.

e- (prefix)

a prefix meaning electronic for current jargon terms, such as e-commerce, e-business and so on.

easter egg

a hidden, undocumented program sequence built into a program that only activates when you press the right keys. They are often funny and they are often used to introduce the team that developed the program. If you are using Netscape, typing about: mozilla into the URL window will give you an example.

e-business

a term that is easily confused with E-Commerce. E-Business may be an umbrella term that refers to any type of business transaction on the Internet. Some writers, however, may use the term in a more restricted context such as a business-to-business (B2B) transaction as opposed to a business-to-consumer (B2C) transaction. For example, a B2B transaction might be a business firm's online banking transaction. E-Commerce refers more to the B2C context where a firm sells goods on the Internet and makes collections via some payment scheme such as online credit card transactions.

e-cash

electronic money designed to be used over a network or stored on cards similar to credit cards. E-cash is still more of an idea than a practical reality, largely due to security concerns.

echo

return response between a host server and a terminal computer. It is generally coded to be 'on' or 'off.' If echo is 'on' (full duplex), the host will send back every character the user types in. If echo is 'off' (half duplex), the host will not send back the characters and the user's local computer or terminal writes each character to the screen directly. This can be confusing to new users if the state of the echo parameter is different on the host computer and the user's computer.

EDGAR

Electronic Data Gathering, Analysis and Retrieval. Database of the Securities and Exchange Commission (SEC). EDGAR contains the digitised versions of many corporate filings, including 10Q quarterly and 10K annual financial reports of registered corporations and mutual funds.

EDI

Electronic Data Interchange or Electronic Data Invoicing. The EDI system allows linked computers to conduct business transactions such as ordering and invoicing over telecommunications networks. The technology dates back to the 1970s when the first attempts at setting uniform standards commenced. However, EDI in telecommunications never lived up to its expectations largely due to high fees of Value Added Network (VAN) providers that, prior to the Internet usage, charged both monthly and transaction fees. In the late 1990s, EDI became less costly (as low as 10% of former VAN costs) when business applications exploded on the Internet and in intranets. The ultimate goal of EDI is to have standardised computer forms for business transactions and networking of nearly all aspects business transactions. This would greatly simplify use of networks to conduct business, accounting for transactions and auditing.

eduquest

a revitalised system of multimedia hardware and software packages from IBM Corporation. The system primarily targets the K-12 education system in the United States. The new system is designed to be more powerful with networked PCs and a variety of Plug and Play adapters for auxiliary components.

e-form

an electronic form that is filled out by a user and sent over a network. They are typically used to place orders or provide feedback. E-forms can be placed on web pages or in Java applets and usually contain text boxes, buttons and other components.

electronic classroom

a large or small classroom filled with multimedia devices. The usual context is that of a lecture hall where the instructor has fingertip control of multimedia aids such as computer images, video tape images, videodisc images, audio, CD-ROM players, Internet connections, cameras that transfer images to large screens, etc. Some electronic classrooms have student response hardware such as response pads or even computer terminals. Usually, however, the electronic classroom is not viewed in the same context as a computer/multimedia lab or a language lab. In a lab setting the student usually works alone or in small teams in front of computers. In an electronic classroom, the instructor is usually focussing the attention of the entire class upon the same learning media. However, labs can be equipped with central screens so that combinations of instructor-focussed materials can be combined with individual learning. Large lecture halls can also be equipped with students who combine large lectures with 'studio classroom learning'.

■ **Electronic Codebook (ECB)**

block cipher mode that consists of simply applying the cipher to blocks of data in sequence, one block at a time.

■ **electronic frontier foundation**

the Electronic Frontier Foundation is a non-profit civil liberties organisation working in the public interest to protect privacy, free expression and access to public resources and information online, as well as to promote responsibility in new media.

■ **e-mail**

Electronic mail. One of the earliest standard Internet protocols which enables people with different computers and operating systems to communicate with each other. E-mail allows one-to-one or one-to-many mailings. Mail is received and held by a mail server within an organisation or by an Internet service provider until the addressee logs on to collect the mail. The Internet e-mail standards include no provision for authenticating the sender, which makes it possible for spammers to use false From addresses and routing.

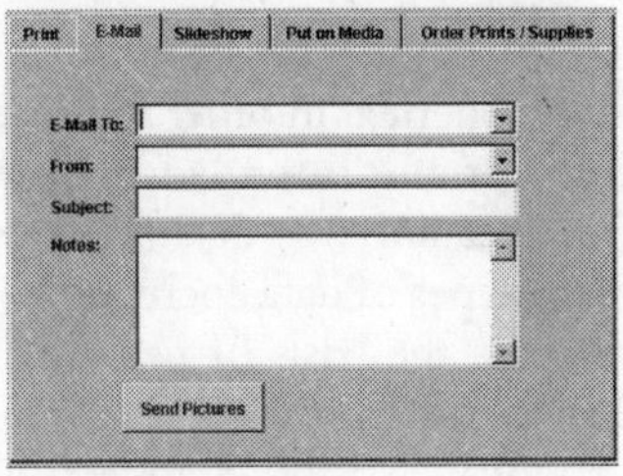

■ **e-mail address**

an electronic mail address. E-mail addresses follow the formula: user-ID@domain-name.

■ **e-mail never-neverland**

a fictitious 'place' where lost e-mail is said to wind up.

■ **e-mail overload**

the state of being completely overwhelmed by the amount of e-mail one has received.

■ **emoticon**

a cute sideways face created by using special characters on the keyboard. Used to express emotions without words. For example, this winking face ,-) indicates 'I'm joking', this sad face :-(expresses sadness or 'I'm sulking'. If this makes no sense, turn your head sideways and look again. Also known as a 'smiley'.

■ **Encapsulating Security Payload (ESP)**

IPSEC header that encrypts the contents of an IP packet. The most recent implementations of IPSEC may also provide authentication and anti-replay protection of the AH to the packets.

■ encryption

cryptographic conversion of data into ciphertext in order to prevent any but the intended recipient from reading that data. There are many types of data encryption and they are the basis of network security. Common types include Data Encryption Standard and public-key encryption.

■ entering wedge

weakness in a crypto system or other security system that gives an attacker a way to break down some of the system's protections.

■ enterprise

a synonym for business, mainly big business. The enterprise computing market is typically the corporations that buy hardware and software and use them to run their operations.

■ entry page

see **gateway page**.

■ EPG

Electronic Program Guide that displays scheduled shows on screen such as TV Guide on Screen.

■ ERIC

Educational Resources Information Centre documents database that contains a variety of resources to educators, especially teachers in K-12 schools.

■ Escrowed Encryption Standard (EES)

standard developed by NSA and published by NIST for crypto systems that allows law enforcement and other authorised agencies to tap the encrypted communications by providing a method to recover the crypto keys being used. This standard is not used in any currently available systems or products.

■ ESH

Electronic Super Highway. See **information highway.**

■ Ethernet

a very common method of networking computers in a LAN. There is more than one type of Ethernet. By 2001, the standard type was '100-BaseT' which can handle up to about 100,000,000 bits-per-second and can be used with almost any kind of computer.

■ euroseek

a search engine which concentrates on information relating to Europe. The URL is http://www.euroseek.com.

■ evaluation

see **assessment**.

■ event handler

a special type of function that executes automatically when a particular user-enabled, system-enabled or code-generated event occurs.

■ e-world

a commercial world-wide network launched by Apple Corporation to compete with Interchange, CompuServe, Prodigy and America Online. Key features of e-World include its ease of use and graphical interface. The major limitation is that its use is restricted to Mac operating systems. A second drawback according to a survey report is that e-World uses older technology revised from America Online. See also **Internet** and **America Online**.

■ excite

regarded as one of the best search engines, with an index of 55 million pages. It can be slow to index new sites. The URL is http://www.excite.com. Sites using frames must have a NOFRAMES section in order to be listed. Some spamming has been noticed. Excite previously ignored the DESCRIPTION meta tag, but is now using this in its listings (although the contents do not affect relevancy, which is based mainly on the title and body text). The use of gateway pages and hidden text is allowed. Excite has an audio/video search facility which is a branded.

■ exclusive or

computational operation on bits that adds the two bits together and discards the carry. This is the basis of the Vernam cipher and key splitting.

■ executable contents

data whose contents represent an executable computer program that is capable of modifying persistent data on a host computer.

■ execute

to process or run a computer program.

■ execution flow

the section of code that the application executes, depending on branching decisions.

■ expansion board/slot

see **board**.

■ expert systems

see **artificial Intelligence.**

■ explorer

see **web browsers**.

■ export control

laws and regulations intended to prevent products from being exported when not in the government's interest. Typically, munitions are placed under export control.

■ extension or file extension

in Windows, DOS and some other operating systems, one or several letters at the end of a filename. Filename extensions usually follow a period (dot) and indicate the type of file. For example, this.txt denotes a plain text file, *that.htm* or *that.html* denotes an HTML file. Some common image extensions are picture.jpg or picture.jpeg or picture.bmp or picture.gif

external viewer

a program used for presenting graphics, audio and video files. Programs that allow the viewing of GIF and JPEG files and the hearing of AU files fall into this category.

extranet

an Intranet that is accessible to computers that are not physically part of a company's' own private network, but that is not accessible to the general public, for example to allow vendors and business partners to access a company web site. Often an intranet will make use of a Virtual Private Network. (*VPN.*)

eyeballs

a viewing audience for a WWW site.

facilitated chat

in a facilitated chat, a host or facilitator controls the messages that appear on the chat screen. Usually used when there is a guest speaker. Facilitated chats provide an orderly environment for the guest speaker and ensure that she is not overwhelmed with dozens of questions all being asked at once.

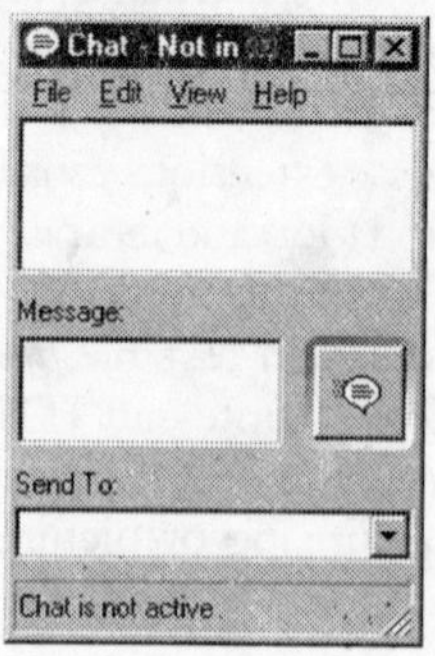

fair use

fair use is the concept in copyright law that some limited copying of copyrighted material is permissible in certain circumstances. A complete work may never be copied. The broadest permissions are for educational purposes, such as copying an article from a magazine or a chapter from a book for a class to use. Other more restrictive permitted uses are short excerpts for purposes of news reporting, criticism and parody.

fake copy listings

sometimes a malicious company will steal a web page or the entire contents of a web site, re-publish at a different URL and register with one or more search engines. This can cause a loss of traffic from the original site if the search engines position the copy higher in the listings. If you find that someone has stolen your site in this way, write to the company concerned and ask them to remove the stolen content. Also contact the hosting service used by the company, any company that benefits from the theft and any search engine(s) concerned. If the thieves refuse to remove the material or ignore you, obtain legal advice. It is also well worth having printed evidence to support your claim that your copy of the material was there first and that you have the copyright!

false drop

a web page retrieved from a search engine or directory which

is not relevant to the query used. This could be for one of the following reasons:
The web page contained the keywords entered, but used in the wrong context, with a different meaning or with a different interrelationship to that expected. The web page is an attempt at spamdexing. The search engine has a fault in its database or a bug in its query program.

■ FAQ

Frequently Asked Questions. A reference document created for particular topic or group that answers to common beginners' questions. It is considered poor Netiquette to ask a question without first reading the FAQ.

■ favorites

in the Internet Explorer browser, a means to get back to a URL you like, similar to Netscape's Bookmarks.

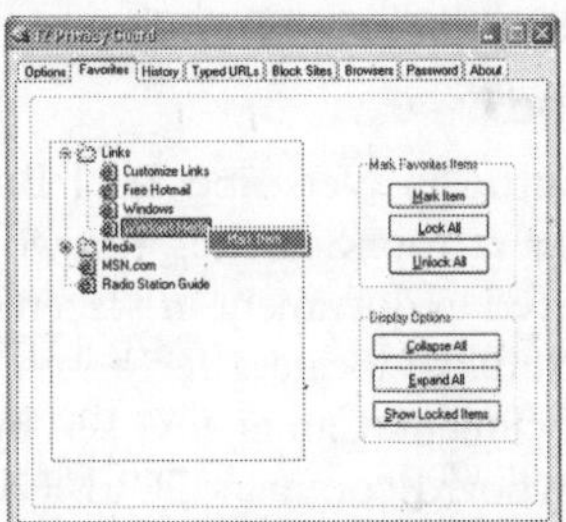

■ fax

devices for transmitting and receiving photocopies over telephone lines. Text and graphics may be printed on paper or stored in computer files. Text is received as a graphic and must be translated by specialised software to be stored as text files for word processors.

■ FDDI

Fibre Distributed Data Interface. A standard for transmitting data on optical fibre cables at a rate of around 100,000,000 bits-per-second (10 time as fast as Ethernet, about twice as fast as *T-3*). See also **bandwidth, Ethernet, T-1, T-3**.

■ FDMA

Frequency Division Multiple Access. It is used in the AMPS system, FDMA is a method of coordinating radio traffic to prevent interference between users sharing a set of frequencies. Only one subscriber can access a given frequency at one time.

■ Federal Information Processing Standard (FIPS)

standards published by NIST that the U. S. government's computer systems should comply with.

■ fibre optic

1. cable that carries light pulses instead of electrical current. A cable comprised of a multitude of

fine glass fibres has much more capacity than the previously popular copper cable.
2. a technology in which light is used to transport information from one point to another. More specifically, fibre optics are thin filaments of glass through which light beams are transmitted over long distances carrying enormous amounts of data.

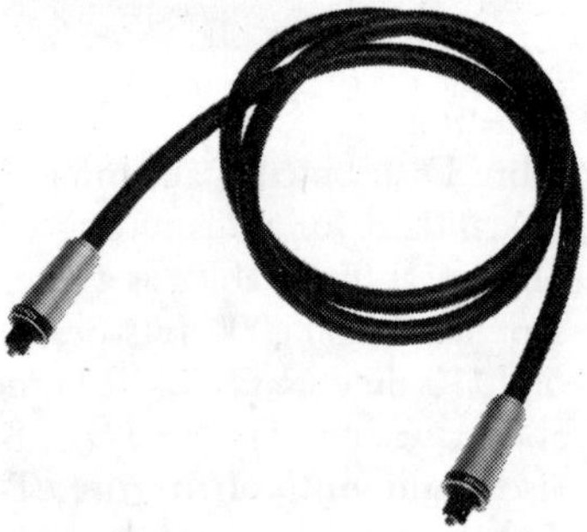

■ fidonet

a worldwide hobbyist network of personal computers started in 1984 that exchanges mail, discussion groups and files.

■ field searching

ability to limit a search by requiring word or phrase to appear in a specific field of documents (e.g., title, URL, link).

■ file attributes

access rights attached to each file.

■ file compression

reducing the size of files for ease of storage and transfer. WinZip is an example of an application that compresses files, the UNIX compress utility is another.

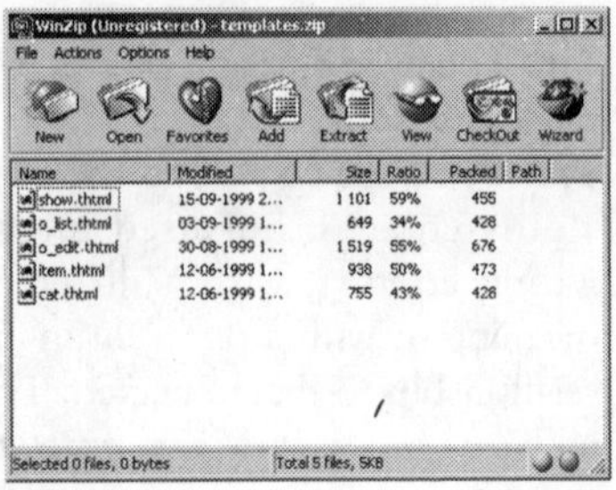

■ file server

a computer running a network operating system that enables other computers to access its files.

■ file transfer

the ability to transfer text, graphics, software, spreadsheets, audio files and video files over vast distances on computer networks such as the Internet. See also **FTP, Internet** and **SLIP.**

■ File Transfer Protocol (FTP)

Internet application and network protocol for transferring files between host computers.

■ find

button in Netscape Tool Button Bar at top. Searches for word(s) keyed in document in screen only. Useful to locate a term in a long document. Can be invoked by the keyboard command, Ctrl + F.

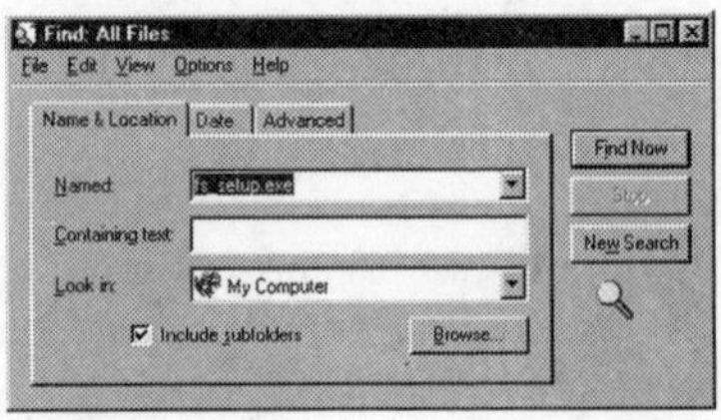

■ finger

an Internet software tool for locating people on other Internet sites. Finger is also sometimes used to give access to non-personal information, but the most common use is to see if a person has an account at a particular Internet site. Many sites do not allow incoming Finger requests, but many do.

■ finger gateway

a source listing of graphics images that have been placed around the world on the Internet.

■ firewall

firewall refers to the concept of a security interface or gateway between a closed system or network and the outside Internet that blocks or manages communications in and out of the system. The security may be provided by passwords, authentication techniques, software and hardware.

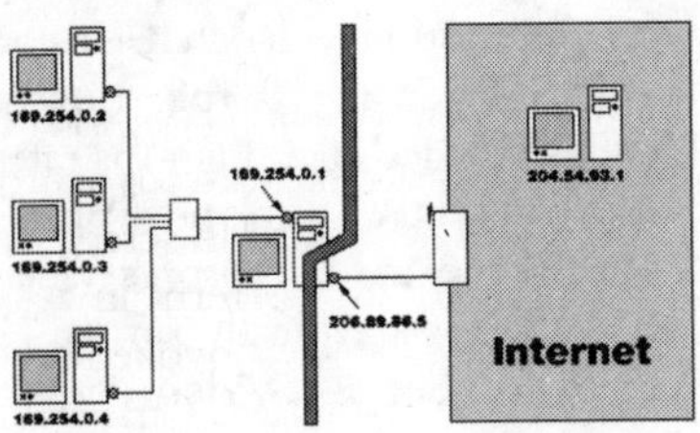

■ flame

personal verbal attacks on other Internet users, via e-mail, USENET or mailing lists. Flame wars occur when a series of flames are sent back and forth between two or more people.

■ flame on/flame off

notifiers that surround a flame message and let readers know that the message they are reading is a flame. Although you don't see these as much as you used to, they would most commonly be used by an individual known to a particular online group who wishes to do a little ranting and then return to the topic at hand.

■ flash memory

an erasable memory used as an alternative to hard disk and laser disc storage. The term is used most often in conjunction with PCMCIA cards.

■ flash session

a feature of America Online that automatically performs online tasks at a designated time. Flash sessions are often used to send/receive e-mail and download large files.

■ flatbed

see **scanner.**

■ flat-file

1. as a noun, an ASCII text file consisting of records of a single type, in which there is no embedded structure information governing relationships between records. 2. as an adjective, describes a flattened representation of a database as single file from which the structure could implicitly be rebuilt.

■ flc/fli

file extensions for animations conforming to Autodesk formats.

With appropriate changes in the win.ini file, most PC computers will play back these animations without having Autodesk software installed. See also **animation.**

■ FM synthesis

the least-expensive method for producing synthesised sound. FM synthesis uses one sine wave to control the frequency of another. Most synthesisers built into PC audio boards and sound modules use more sophisticated synthesis techniques for greater accuracy in reproducing the sounds of different instruments.

■ FMV

Full Motion Video depicting video at 30 or more fps. See also **Video.**

■ font

a typographic style used to display or print characters. Times Roman, Courier and Helvetica are three examples.

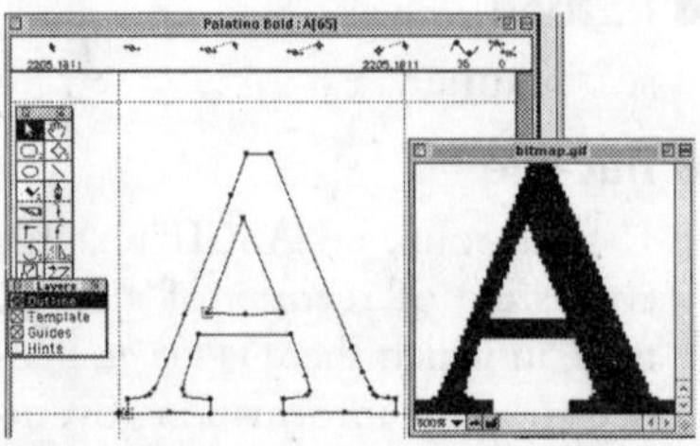

■ font and background spoofs

various techniques used to place invisible text in a web page, to improve positioning without affecting the appearance of the page. These are mostly based on setting the font and background colours to the same value (e.g. white). Most search engines now detect these tricks.

■ forgery

data item whose contents misleads the recipient to believe the item and its contents were produced by someone other than the actual author.

■ fortezza

PC card (formerly called PCMCIA cards) containing the SKIPJACK encryption algorithm and providing crypto services needed to support e-mail applications.

■ forum

a topically-focussed discussion group or area. From the traditional Roman forum.

■ forwarding

sending an e-mail message or post from one person to a third party.

■ fps

frames per second in video. Typical 'full-motion' video in television and movies is 30 fps, but in digitised video such high fps rates are not yet common. Apple's QuickTime and Microsoft's Video for Windows typically run at 12 to 18 fps. See also **video.**

■ frame

1. an HTML feature that allows web designers to segment the window of a web browser into distinct sections.

2. a single complete picture in a moving picture sequence.

frame relay

a packet switching standard based on the older X.25 protocol that achieves greater speeds with fast, reliable networks. It lowers overhead by reducing the accounting and checking procedures used in X.25.

freenets

bulletin board services that are funded by individuals and organisations dedicated to making information freely available on networks. They operate much like public libraries through the National Public Telecommunication Network (NPTN.). Users can connect through modems or through Internet terminals.

freeware

shareware that is openly available to the public without the requirement of user registration fee.

Frequently Hopping Spread Spectrum (FHSS)

a spread spectrum technique that uses a range of frequencies and changes frequencies during the transmission, the technology employed in HomeRF (SWAP) implementations.

freshness

how up-to-date a search engine database is, based primarily on how often its spiders recirculate around the Web and update their copies of the web pages they hold and discover new ones. Also determined by how quickly they integrate new sites that web authors send to them. Two weeks is about as good as most search engines do, but some update certain selected web sites more frequently.

fried

to be totally destroyed or otherwise unusable, as in 'my hard drive is fried' or 'the network is totally fried'.

FTP

File Transfer Protocol. A very common method of moving files between two Internet sites. FTP is a special way to *login* to another Internet site for the purposes of retrieving and/or sending files. There are many Internet sites that have established publicly accessible repositories of material that can be obtained using FTP, by logging in using the account name 'anonymous', thus these sites are called 'anonymous ftp servers'.

fud

abbreviation for Fear, Uncertainty and Doubt. A set of sales tactics employed by market leaders to cast aspersion on competing products. Computer products are often purchased on the basis of perceived market leadership because no one wants to get stuck with a losing product that might not be supported in the near future. The usefulness of using FUD to confuse a market is epitomised by the apocryphal saying, 'No one ever got fired for buying IBM'. A good example of FUD is Microsoft's tactic of pre-announcing products far in advance of their actual availability. All of a sudden the market for competing products evaporates as customers await a dominating Microsoft product.

■ **full-duplex**

in full duplex communication, the terminal transmits and receives data simultaneously.

■ **function**

an instruction to the application that performs operations or returns a value or both.

■ **funding**

the raising of funds for hardware, software and development. Grants are available from a variety of sources. Funding grants are available from a variety of sources tracked in the newsletters.

■ **fuzzy and**

in ranking of results, documents with all terms (Boolean AND) are ranked first, followed by documents containing any terms (Boolean OR) are retrieved. The farther down, the fewer the terms, although at least one should always be present.

■ **FWIW**

acronym for 'For What It's Worth'

■ **FYI**

abbreviation for 'For Your Information'.

■ **GA**

chat shorthand for 'go ahead', frequently used to signify that the person is through typing.

■ **gainmomentum**

the high-end $10,000 hypertext and hypermedia authoring software package from Sybase (800-879-2273).

■ **games**

interactive entertainment programs that can be played back on computers or special playing machines connected to television sets. Some games are sold on compact discs that can either be played in CD-ROM drives connected to computers or CD players that are proprietary. Games are generally authored by game vendors and cannot be modified or updated for education uses by users. Educators who think that their students are spending many hours in computer labs for academic purposes may discover that a large portion of computer lab time is taken up with game playing. More research needs to be conducted on the fascination of games so that educators can make better use of building these motivational factors into more serious learning materials. According to a survey report, CD-ROM games are overtaking market leaders that captured the early game markets with players that were not compatible with PC, Mac or other desktop computers. Games are popular and addictive, in part, due to the release of endorphins in the brain, especially among women. See also **MUDs.**

■ garbage

1. a string of unwanted, meaningless or unintelligible characters produced by error.
2. incorrect input to a computer. See **GIGO**.

■ gateways

are connectors between two or more dissimilar networks that facilitate communication in such instances. Gateways have their own processors to perform both protocol and bandwidth conversions. Gateways between the Outernet and the Internet translate different protocols such as e-mail protocols of different networks into Internet protocols.

■ GDI

Graphics Device Interfaces link graphics hardware devices with the CPU. Much of the power of graphics processing depends upon whether the system has 8-bit, 16-bit, 32-bit or 64-bit graphics power. Limitations of customer hardware often detract from the ability to develop operating systems to take full advantage of graphics power. For example, when developing Windows Chicago for 32-bit processors, Microsoft Corporation had to leave 16-bit GDI capacity on its 32-bit operating system.

■ gershwin

the name given to Apple's planned operating system 9.0 for Mac and PowerPC computers. New features were to include advanced speed recognition, interfacing that adapts to individual users and new microkernal architecture. However, the System 9.0 has been abandoned in favour of an entirely new operating system called Rhapsody. Apple's hopes are riding heavily upon the evolution of a new operating system called Rhapsody that is a revolutionary operating system based upon NEXTStep technology.

■ get a real computer!

an imperative issued as a response to someone who is complaining about not being able to get work done on an obsolete, single-tasking, graphical or otherwise lame computer. Generally, UNIX systems are considered to be real computers in opposition to Windows-based systems.

■ gif

'Graphical Interchange Format' is a commonly used graphics file format for image files on the Internet. A bitmap graphical format originally developed for CompuServe that is widely used in WWW pages. It is particularly good for text art, cartoon art, poster art and line drawings- -all types with solid colours and distinct lines or borders between different colours. GIF files use a .gif extension.

■ gigabyte

1000 or 1024 Megabytes, depending on who is measuring.

■ GIGO

acronym for Garbage In Garbage Out. Usually said in response to complaints that a program didn't 'do the right thing' when given bad or flawed input. See **garbage**.

■ gina

a graphical interface (formerly known as GUIDE) for the Internet. This is a low-cost option for graphically interfacing with e-mail, bulletin boards, databases, library catalogues, news services and conferencing.

■ glitch

a small malfunction.

■ GMT

Greenwich Mean Time. Often used as a standard time zone. In e-mail headers, you will often see references to the hours offset from GMT. For example, Eastern Standard Time is GMT minus 5 hours because of the 5 hour difference between Greenwich, England and the Eastern US.

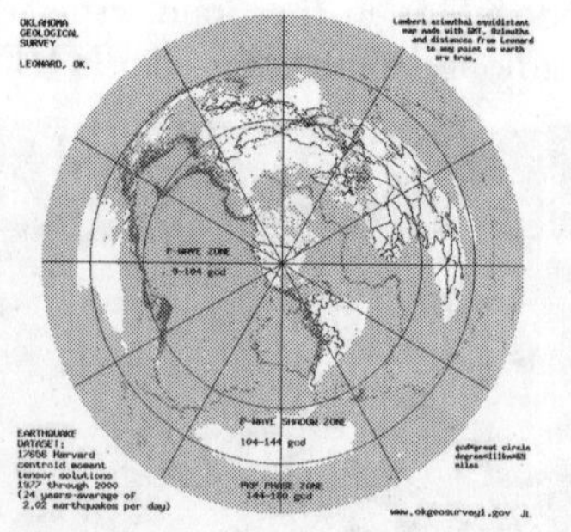

■ GMTA

chat shorthand for 'Great Minds Think Alike'.

■ go

button in Netscape Menu Bar at top. Provides list of recent sites you visited, retained for the current session only. Click on any site in the list to return to the site. For a more permanent marker, make a Bookmark.

■ go word

the word associated with a forum or area on a commercial online service that allows you to get to that place quickly.

■ go.com

a portal partnership between Infoseek and Disney, with search capabilities based on the Infoseek index, at http://go.com/.

■ golden rule of netiquette

'Remember the Human', the rule upon which all Netiquette is based. Often in electronic communications, it is easy to forget that you are communicating with real people, not just networks of computers. See **netiquette**.

gopher

invented at the University of Minnesota in 1993 just before the Web, gopher was a widely successful method of making menus of material available over the Internet. Gopher was designed to be much easier to use than FTP, while still using a text-only interface. Gopher is a Client and Server style program, which requires that the user have a Gopher Client program. Although Gopher spread rapidly across the globe in only a couple of years, it has been largely supplanted by Hypertext, also known as WWW (World Wide Web).

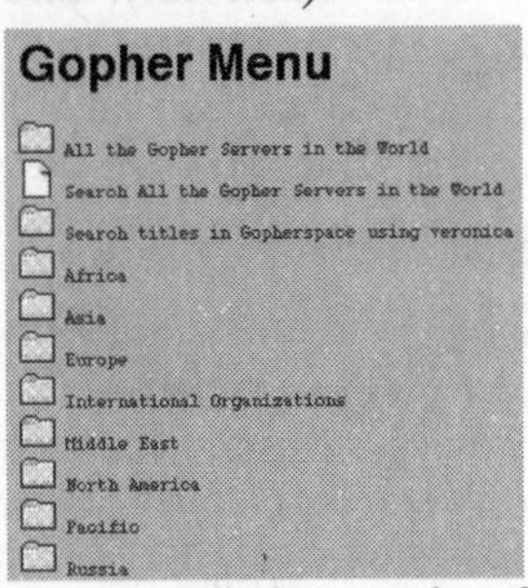

There are still thousands of Gopher Servers on the Internet and we can expect they will remain for a while.

gopherspace

a term used to describe the entire gopher network.

goto

a search engine, powered by Inktomi, which only returns one URL per domain in its search results. Operates a 'pay per click' scheme where websites can pay to increase their relevancy. The URL is http://www.goto.com.

GPF

General Protection Fault. The curse of Windows!

GPS

Global Positioning System hardware that facilitates navigation via satellites. There are now versions for automobiles that have LCD screens to show maps and present vehicle location.

grants

see **funding**.

graphics

computer images that contain pictures, drawings and other

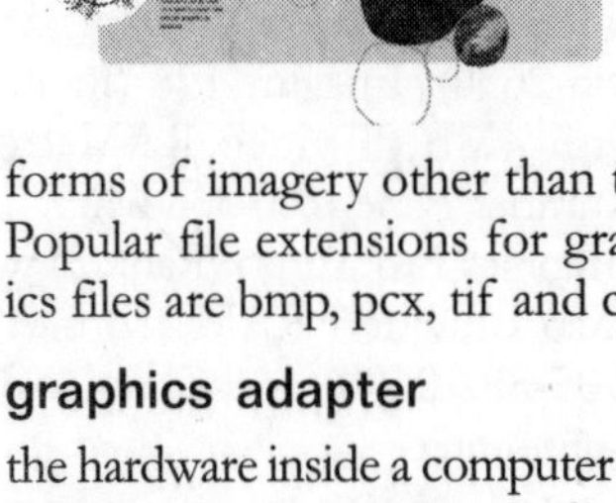

forms of imagery other than text. Popular file extensions for graphics files are bmp, pcx, tif and cgm.

graphics adapter

the hardware inside a computer that enables the computer to display graphics on the screen. In contrast to Mac computers, PCs have a larger variety of graphics adapters that complicate compatibility between different PCs. In the early days, the PC standard was the Colour Graphics Adapter (CGA) that, by today's standards, is low resolution and low in colour combinations. This was replaced by EGA Enhanced Graphics Adapter and then VGA Video Graphics Array having a standard 480 lines vertical and 640 pixels horizontal resolution. Today Super VGA extensions (to at least 600 lines vertical and 800 pixels horizontal) are the choice among most PC users for whom graphics displays are important. Be aware, however, that there are different Super VGA resolutions and monitor options that can affect the compatibility of graphics images among different PCs. Also be aware that LCD panels are not able to handle the higher resolutions of cathode ray monitors, therefore, images may not look as good during class delivery as they did on a monitor during the authoring process. The top-rated graphics adapters at the end of 1994 are Impression Plus (Rank 1) with 4Mb of video RAM from Matrox (514-685-2630), Imagine-128 (Rank 2) with 4Mb of video RAM from Number Nine (800-438-6463) and Graphics Pro Turbo (Rank 3) with 4Mb of video RAM from ATI (905-882-2600) according to PC Computing.

■ **grep**

1. to rapidly scan a large volume of information looking for a particular string or pattern.
2. a UNIX command used to scan a file or group of files for a matching search string or pattern.

■ **griefer**

an online game role player who sabotages the game by harassing, deceiving, cheating, robbing or killing newer players.

■ **group**

a collection of users.

■ **group rights**

rights given to a collection of users.

■ **groupware**

software applications that facilitate shared work over long distances on documents and information. Groupware supports person-to-person collaborations and includes Lotus, Livelink from Open Text Intranets, E-mail, Silent Meeting Systems, Videocon-ferencing, etc.

■ **GSM**

Global System for Mobile Communications. A variant of TDMA, GSM is the closest to a worldwide standard for cellular service. A single-frequency GSM cellular handset may work compatibly in Europe, Asia, India and Africa—though not in the United States.

■ **hacker**

1. originally, a hacker was a term of respect among computer designers, programmers and engineers for those among them who created truly original and ingenious programs, devices or sometimes very clever practical jokes.
2. unfortunately, the current popular meaning of the term is to describe those who break into sys-

tems, destroy data, steal copyrighted software and perform other destructive or illegal acts with computers and networks.

■ handle

a nickname used in online communications.

■ handshaking

a set of commands recognised by the sending and receiving stations that control the flow of data transmission.

■ hang

1. an unexpected halt of a computer, usually while running an application program. A hung machine is characterised by a total lack of response from the mouse and keyboard. The user can almost never affect a recovery except by turning the computer off and restarting it.
2. in the construction 'hang off', to attach a peripheral device to a computer via a cable. 'I'm going to hang another hard drive off my home box'.

■ hard drive

a 'hard disc' file storage disc (usually a magnetic disc) on a computer that has higher storage capacity and faster access time (e.g., under 20 ms) than slower devices such as floppy disc drives and optical disc (e.g., CD-ROM) drives. This is not the same as memory or random access memory (RAM). Usually the term 'hard drive' refers to rigid discs coated with magnetic material.

■ hardwired

a function or capability that is hardcoded into a system. Generally, anything that cannot be modified or customised.

■ hash

improved checksum in which it is hard for someone to construct a data block that generates a predetermined checksum or hash value.

■ Hawthorne effects

refer to distortions and possibly non-sustaining effects of a treatment just because its newness captures more of an individual's attentiveness. In double blind studies of the impact of technologies upon learning, Hawthorne effects are particularly troublesome. Students are more apt to be more attentive to newer technologies simply because they are 'new' curiosities. Positive results on learning impacts may not be sustaining, however, after the novelty and curiosity factors decline with repeated use of the technology over time.

■ HDTV

High-Definition TV in digitised formats that will eventually replace present analog formats in 16:9 wide-screen TV. The Japanese version of HDTV is not truly the fully digitised version broadcast system intended for the United States by the end of the year 2000.

■ head or header (of html document)

the top portion of the HTML source code behind Web pages, beginning with <HEAD> and ending with </HEAD>. It contains the Title, Description, Keywords fields and others that web page authors may use to describe the page. The title appears in the title bar of most browsers, but the other fields cannot be seen as part of the body of the page. To view the <HEAD> portion of web pages in Netscape, click VIEW, Page Source. In Internet Explorer, click View, Source. Some search engines will retrieve based on text in these fields.

■ heading

many search engines give extra weight and importance to the text found inside HTML heading sections. It is generally considered good advice to use headings when designing web pages and to place keywords inside headings.

■ hertz

unit of measure that equals a frequency of one cycle per second. See also **bandwidth**, **bps**, **kilohertz** and **megahertz**.

■ hex, hexadecimal

base 16 arithmetic. Conventionally, the 16 digits are represented by the digits 0 through 9 and the letters A through F. The letter A, for example, represents the decimal number 10. A byte (8 bits of data) is often represented by two hexadecimal numbers. The hexadecimal values can range from 00 to FF or from decimal 0 to 255. Hexadecimal values are often differentiated from decimal by either following them with the letter h or preceding them with an angle bracket, for example 33h or >0B. Hexadecimal numbers have many applications in computer programming and they are frequently used in RGB (red/green/blue) colour coding for web pages.

■ hidden text

text on a web page which is visible to search engine spiders but not visible to human visitors. This is sometimes because the text has been set the same colour as the background, because multiple Title tags have been used or because the text is an HTML comment. Hidden text is often used for spamdexing. Many search engines can now detect the use of hidden text and often remove offending pages from their database or lower such pages' positioning. Text can also be hidden using agent name delivery or IP delivery either to present different text to different search engine spiders or to hide the real HTML source from competitors.

■ high risk application

computer application in which the enterprise operating it can suffer a significant loss through a computer security incident.

■ hijacking

attack in which the attacker takes over a live connection between two entities so that the attacker can masquerade as one of the entities.

■ history, search history

available• by using the combined keystrokes CTRL + H, a more permanent record of sites you have visited/retrieved than GO. You can set how many days your Netscape retains history in Edit | Preferences and in Internet Explorer in Tools | Internet Options-General.

■ hit

1. in search terminology, every listing a search engine returns from a search is called a hit.

2. the term hit is also used to refer to calls on a web server and it is much misunderstood. Technically, if a web page is called by a remote browser and it includes three graphics, there are four hits on that server, one for the page and one for each graphic. Many people and most 'hit counters' use the term hit to mean hits on the web page only, not the calls to graphics or other supporting files that come with the page. When someone quotes figures on hits, be aware that definitions and uses vary and try to find out what definition was used in producing the figures.

■ HL

Hyper-Learning using hypertext, hypermedia and computer networks. Authors tend to use the term in the context of learning from servers on an information highway such as the Internet after multimedia transmissions become more common.

■ hoax

there are many hoaxes continually popping up on the nets. False viruses are the most common of these with names like 'Join the Crew' or 'PenPal Greetings', but there are many more themes that keep recurring. Appeals to charity is a common theme for a hoax, sometimes partially based in fact. There are also lots of stories going around about Bill Gates and moneymaking schemes and expensive cookie recipes and stolen kidneys, all of which are interesting stories, but usually false or even fraudulent.

■ holy wars

ubiquitous online disputes that never end. Common holy wars are fought over Macintosh vs. Windows, UNIX vs. Windows NT and everyone vs. Microsoft, as well as over societal issues such as abortion, gun control and pornography. See also **flame war**.

■ homepage

a web page that is topically the main source of information about a particular person, group or concept. Many people on the web create home pages about themselves for fun, these are also known as vanity pages.

hop

a message or data packet travels a path among routers on a network through a series of hops from the source to the destination.

host

1. a computer that allows users to communicate with other host computers on a network.
2. a chat term for someone who is managing a chat. Hosts often act as referees and have the power to turn participants into spectators and vice versa.

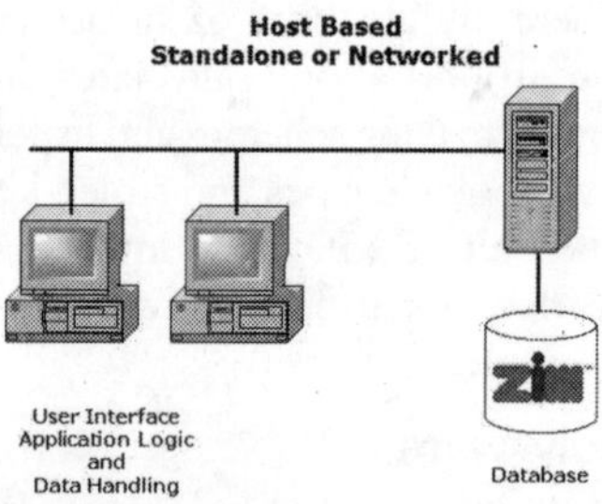

host address

the address used by others on the network to communicate with a particular host.

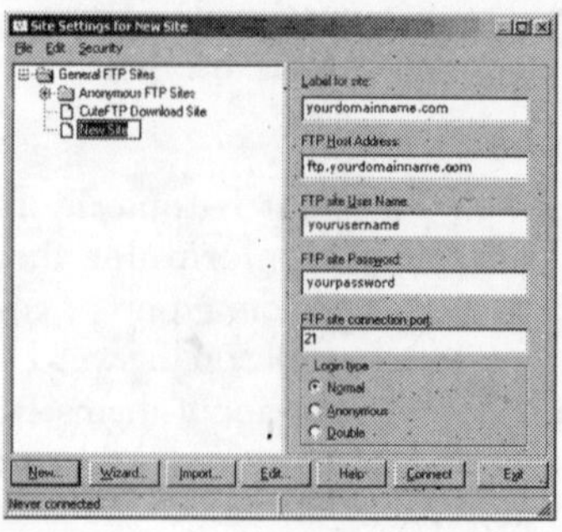

hot list

similar to a bookmark in Gopher or Netscape, this list makes note of particular pages on the WWW that are accessed when using the Mosaic browser.

hot spots

buttons or other programmable objects that can activate objects or linked events.

hotbot

one of the largest search engines, indexing 110 million pages. Powered by Inktomi, new submissions appear to be taking two weeks or longer to appear. The URL is http://www.hotbot.com.

hotlink

see **hyperlink.**

hotword

see **hyperlink**.

HP/UX

Hewlett-Packard Unix Operating System. Hewlett-Packard also uses other operating systems such as its own proprietary MPE and NEXTStep. See also **operating system** and **Unix.**

HTML

Hypertext Markup Language. A standardised language of computer code, imbedded in 'source' documents behind all Web documents, containing the textual content, images, links to other documents (and possibly other applications such as sound or motion) and formatting instructions for display on the screen. When you view a Web page, you are looking at the product of this code working behind the scenes in conjunction with your browser. Browsers are programmed to interpret HTML for display. HTML often imbeds within it other programming languages and applications such as SGML, XML, Javascript, CGI-script and more. It is possible to deliver or access and execute virtually any program via the WWW. You can see HTML in Netscape by selecting the View pop-down menu tab, then 'Document Source.' If you download a document as 'Source', the file will contain HTML markup codes and can be viewed in Netscape and other browsers.

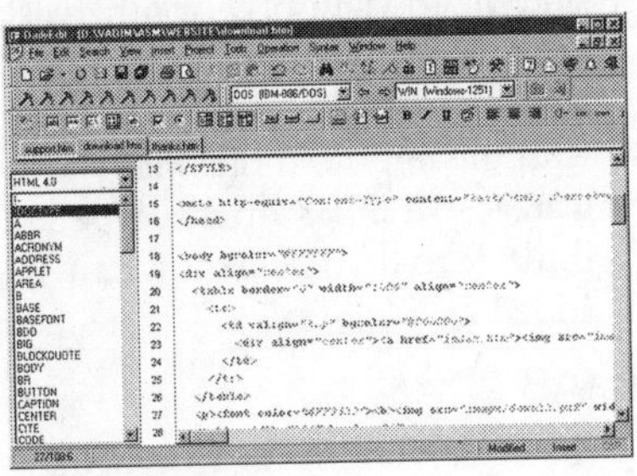

■ HTML document

a document with a Hypertext Markup Language DTD. It must be read using HTTP protocol.

■ HTTP

Hyper Text Transfer Protocol. Often this is the initial sequence of letters in a web address. It is the main protocol used on the World Wide Web that enables linking to other web sites.

■ hub

a device that connects the cables from computers and other devices such as printers in an ethernet local area network. Traditionally, hubs are used for star topology networks, but they are often used with other configurations to make it easy to add and remove computers without bringing down the network. Smart hubs or switching hubs are often used to improve performance by managing traffic.

■ Hx-Pro

an audio tape monitoring system marketed by a renowned company that facilitates recording of analog audio tapes at higher decibel levels to reduce tape hiss. This is a feature available on high-end tape decks.

■ hype

marketing messages that overstate the truth (as in 'Don't believe the hype!').

■ hypercard

see **hypermedia, hypertext, world wide web**.

hyperfacts

hypertext and/or hypermedia versions of fact books. The best known of these are encyclopaedia CD-ROMs.

hyperfiction

hypertext and/or hypermedia versions of fiction, usually on CD-ROM discs. The main feature of hyperfiction is that alternative navigations through the plot are possible. In some cases the reader creatively determines certain outcomes.

hyperlink

a link in a web page that brings you to another location or resource when activated. Hyperlinks usually appear as underlined text and printed in a contrasting colour, but they may also appear as graphics, such as buttons to click. Hyperlinks may link to another place in the same page, to a different page, to play an audio or video file, to download a file, to set up a message to an e-mail address, to search a database, to read Usenet newsgroups and to link to other Internet resources.

hypermedia

hypertext with added features for audio and video features. Hypermedia may also entail touchscreen or remote control capabilities such that users can navigate by touching the computer screen or remote control devices. Eventually hypermedia will entail other senses such as smell. The key to hypermedia is random access that allows lightning-fast non-linear navigation based upon reader choice or other reader actions such as responses to questions. The term 'multimedia' is not totally synonymous with 'hypermedia' because multimedia may not entail hypertext authoring.

hypertext

on the World Wide Web, the feature, built into HTML, that allows a text area, image or other object to become a 'link' (as if in a chain) that retrieves another computer file (another Web page, image, sound file or other document) on the Internet. The range of possibilities is limited by the ability of the computer retrieving the outside file to view, play or otherwise open the incoming file. It needs to have software that can interact with the imported file. Many software capabilities of this type are built into browsers or can be added as 'plug-ins'.

IAB

the abbreviation for Internet Architecture Board. The IAB is the council that makes decisions about Internet standards. See also **IETF**.

IANA

Internet Assigned Numbers Authority

ICANN

Internet Corporation for Assigned Names and Numbers

■ **icon**

a small graphic image that represents a file or application and when clicked upon produces a programmed result.

■ **iconographer**

a skilful designer who elevates icon design to an art form.

■ **IDE**

Intelligent Drive Electronics. Interface hard drive disc controller standard for PCs that enables the controller to reside on the motherboard and, thereby, not require the use of an expansion slot. This enhances ease of installation and allows for the elimination of SCSI controllers for accessing auxiliary hard drives, CD-ROM drives, CD-R drives, etc.

■ **identity hacking**

posing as someone else. Posting anonymously or pseudonymously, usually with the intent to deceive.

■ **IDL**

Interface Definition Language. It facilitates interfacing between servers and IDL compliant client computers. For example, a Java IDL enables Java to communicate with non-Java objects on networks.

■ **IDTV**

Improved Definitional TV that uses a computerised line doubling technique to simulate HDTV at higher resolutions. See also **video** and **HDTV**.

■ **IEEE**

Institute for Electrical and Electronics Engineers, a professional organisation which sets standards for telecommunications and computers.

■ **IETF**

Internet Engineering Task Force. IETF refers to a subgroup of the Internet Architecture Board that focuses on solving technical problems on the Internet.

■ **IIOP**

Internet Inter-orb Protocol. An evolving wire-level protocol that defines how distributed objects communicate with each other. IIOP—which is similar to Microsoft's Distributed Common Object Model (DCOM) specification—is based around the Common Object Request Broker Architecture (CORBA). In theory, any IIOP-compliant client software on any platform will be able to access the same object, a programming function that performs a specific task (such as authenticating a user against a server).

■ **IIRC**

short for 'If I Remember Correctly'.

■ **IKE**

IBM Kiosk for Education.

■ **ILEC**

Incumbent Local Exchange Carrier. See **LEC**

■ image map

a set of hyperlinks attached to areas of an image. This may be defined within a web page or as an external file. If the image map is defined as an external file, search engines may have problems indexing your other pages, unless you duplicate the links as conventional text hyperlinks. If the image map is included within the web page, the search engines should have no problem following the links, although it's good practice to provide text links too, to aid the visually impaired and those accessing the web with graphics switched off or using text only browsers.

■ IMAP

Internet Message Access Protocol (sometimes listed as Internet Mail Access Protocol). A mail protocol that provides management of received messages on a remote server. The user can review headers, create or delete folders/mailboxes and messages and search contents remotely without downloading. It includes more functions than the similar POP protocol.

■ IMHO

shorthand for 'In My Humble Opinion'. Often used in chat and messages by people whose opinion is anything but humble. Sometimes more accurately rendered as IMNSHO (In My Not So Humble Opinion).

■ in line encryptor

product that applies encryption automatically to all data passing along a data link.

■ inbound link

a hypertext link to a particular page from elsewhere, bringing traffic to that page. Inbound links are counted to produce a measure of the page popularity. Searches for the inbound links to a page can be made on Altavista, Infoseek and Hotbot.

■ inbox

a folder where you receive incoming mail.

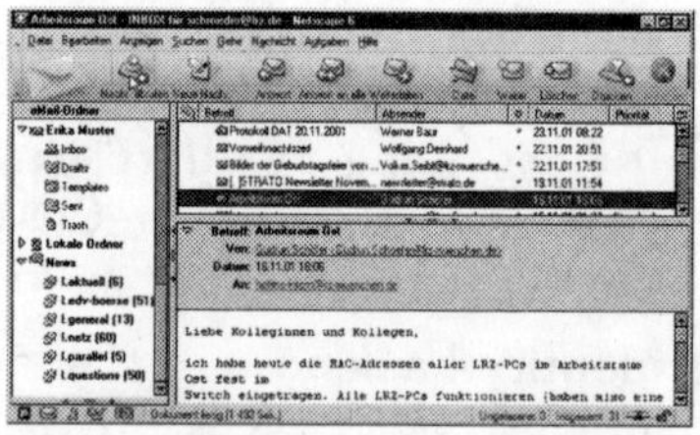

■ incremental packet writing

like multisession Photo CD, this process lets you add data to a disk in multiple sessions and create a single table of contents when the disk is full. Unlike Photo CD disks, though, a disk written in this way is readable by other CD drives only when the disk is finalised, not before. See also **CD-R.**

■ indeo

video compression hardware manufactured by Intel for PC computers. The i750 chipset will capture 32-by-240 pixel windows at 15 fps and 160-by-120 pixel windows at 30 fps. Creative Labs (that markets the popular Sound Blaster and Video Blaster hardware/software) will now market the Indeo boards. The main competitor for Indeo will be MPEG compression boards that are anticipated by analysts to be the major standard of the future.

■ index

it refers to the database of web pages maintained by a search engine or directory.

■ Industry, Scientific and Medical (ISM) band

an unregulated radio frequency that uses the 900 MHz and 2.4 GHz bands for communication, these bands were approved by the FCC in 1985.

■ infind

a meta search engine. Found at http://www.infind.com.

■ infobahn

a variant of information superhighway.

■ information highway

a world wide combination of fibre optic cable and satellite receivers in a future time when homes and offices around the world will be linked by highways of electronic information that can be traversed interactively both to and from a connected user.

■ Information Security (INFOSEC)

technical security measures that involve communications security, cryptography and computer security.

■ infoseek

one of the largest search engines. New sites are normally added very quickly, within one or two business days. The URL is http://www.infoseek.com. Infoseek is one of the few search engines to treat singular and plural forms as the same word. Very sensitive to page popularity in its positioning algorithm.

■ inktomi

the database used by some of the largest search engines, including Hotbot. Inktomi is also used by Yahoo when no matches are found in Yahoo's own database.

■ inline images

these are the graphics contained within a Web document.

■ inlining

the practice of putting an IMG tag in a web page that calls a graphic from another site. Many sites, particularly those offering free storage, now view this as bandwidth theft and block remote IMG calls from other sites to their site. It is particularly bad netiquette and very likely a copyright violation to display a graphic called from someone else's web page.

■ instant messaging

messaging between to or more individuals who are simultaneously online. It is more like a telephone conversation than e-mail.

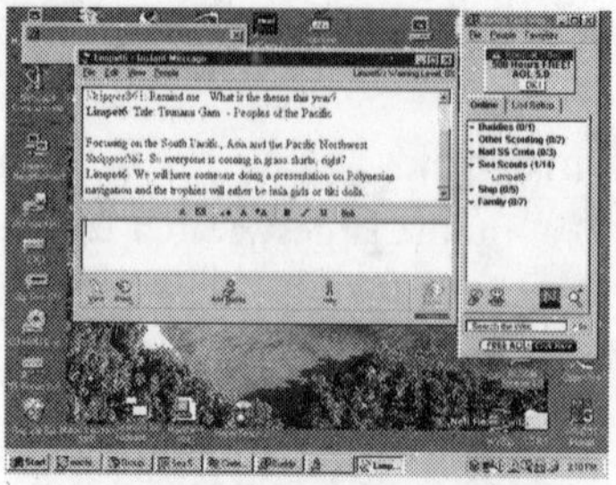

■ **Integrated Services Digital Network (ISDN)**

a technology offered by telephone carriers that allows for the rapid transfer of voice and data.

■ **integrity**

the ability to ensure that information is not modified except by people who are explicitly intended to modify it.

■ **intellectual property**

the concept of legal protection for original creations. It encompasses copyright, trademarks and patents.

■ **interactive TV**

see **information highway.**

■ **intercast**

a term given by Intel Corporation for incoming-only (push-only) reception of HDTV. An upgrade tuner for intercasting can be installed in a PC. The cost of such a tuner is under $150. Without any monthly fee, phone modem or cable modem, users can receive broadcasts and webcasts. However, intercasting will not allow interactive searching or other two-way communication. See also **HDTV** and **webcasting**.

■ **interchange**

a commercial network service introduced by a computer book publishing firm called Ziff-Davis. Although designed to compete with CompuServe and other commercial network services, Interchange tries to provide more services for technology monitoring of computer users.

■ **interface**

the connection between a computer and its auxiliary equipment such as hard drives, CD-ROM drives, videodisc players, printers, scanners, etc.

■ **interleaving**

a process that allows separate channels for data, audio and video files to be played back simultaneously on a compact disc. Interleaving also allows the reader to choose from one of several audio channels while a video channel is playing. In playback, interleaved audio and video sequences are alternately played back such that on slow systems there may be choppy interrupts when video and audio are played simultaneously.

■ **International Data Encryption Algorithm (IDEA)**

block cipher developed in Switzerland and used in PGP.

■ **International Internet Association (IIA)**

an Internet service that may be accessed for a fee under instructions given at phone number 813-

923-4093. The IIA taps over 20,000 databases worldwide, including databases from government, business firms, news services and universities.

■ International Standards Organisation (ISO)

International organisation that published a large number of networking standards (the OSI protocols), most of which are incompatible with the Internet protocols. Protocols originally developed by the CCITT are generally ISO protocols.

■ internaut

slang for someone who is an experienced Internet user.

■ Internet

a worldwide network of networks that all use the TCP/IP communications protocol and share a common address space. First incarnated as the ARPANET in 1969, the Internet has metamorphosed from a military Internet work to an academic research Internet work to the current commercial Internet work. It commonly supports services such as e-mail, the World Wide Web, file transfer and Internet Relay Chat. The Internet is experiencing tremendous growth in the number of users, hosts and domain names. It is gradually subsuming other media, such as proprietary computer networks, newspapers, books, television and the telephone. Also known as 'the net', 'the information superhighway' and 'cyberspace'.

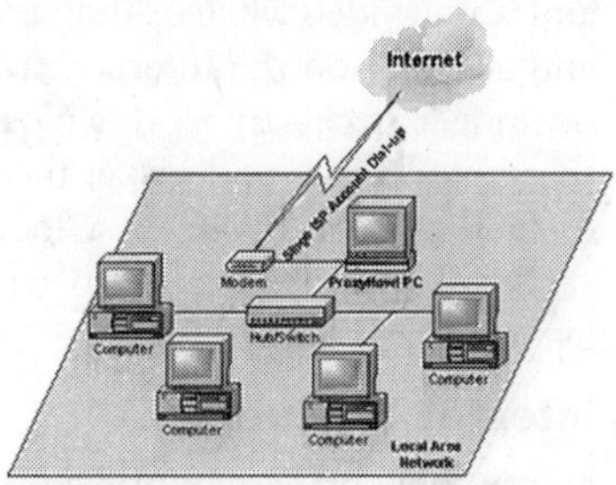

■ Internet 2

the Internet 2 Consortium of more than 100 universities and other organisations collaborating to develop the next-generation Internet technology. In addition to bandwidth issues, the Consortium is dealing with such issues as audio and video integration, interactive distance learning, telemedicine, online research collaboration and real-time simulation/modelling.

■ Internet address (a.k.a. IP address)

an assigned series of numbers unique to each computer on the Internet which is used to identify it for data exchanges.

■ Internet Address and Numbering Authority (IANA)

administrative organisation that assigns host addresses and other numeric constants used in the Internet protocols.

Internet audio and video

the transport of audio and video such that users can hear sounds and watch video while reading text and graphics on the Internet. It is no longer necessary to download these media files and install them on a local computer or a local server. These files can be played live on the Internet.

Internet Explorer (IE)

a free web browser application from Microsoft.

Internet Key Exchange (IKE)

key management protocol IPSEC based on ISAKMP and tailored for typical Internet applications.

Internet messaging

technologies for sending messages across the Internet.

Internet phones and videoconferencing

emerging telephony on the Internet coupled with the extension to video telephony.

Internet Relay Chat (IRC)

a chat network that operates over the Internet. Originally evolved from the UNIX talk program, IRC is similar to the chat systems found on commercial online services.

Internet Security Association Key Management Protocol (ISAKMP)

key management application protocol for IPSEC that has been endorsed by the IETF as a required part of any complete IPSEC implementation.

Internet Service Provider (ISP)

1. a business that delivers access to the Internet, usually for a monthly fee. There are thousands of ISPs all around the world.
2. any business that provides Internet services such as web sites or web site development.

Internet Society (ISOC)

to quote its home page at http://info.isoc.org: 'The Internet Society is a non-governmental International organisation for global cooperation and coordination for the Internet and its Internetworking technologies and applications. The Society's individual and organisational members are bound by a common stake in maintaining the viability and global scaling of the Internet. They comprise the companies, government agencies and foundations that have created the Internet and its technologies as well as innovative new entrepreneurial organisations contributing to maintain that dynamic'.

Internetwork Packet Exchange (IPX)

one of the data transmission protocols used by NetWare.

internic infosource

an information server about the Internet.

■ interoperability

the ability of software and hardware on multiple machines from multiple vendors to communicate meaningfully.

■ intranet

a network of networks that interconnects within a single widespread organisation and uses the Internet Protocol (IP). The sites within an Intranet are generally closed to the Internet and are accessible to organisation members only.

■ IP

the abbreviation for Internet Protocol, IP refers to the set of communication standards that control communications activity on the Internet. An IP address is the number assigned to any Internet-connected computer.

■ IP delivery

similar to agent name delivery, this technique presents different content depending on the IP address of the client. It is very difficult to view pages hidden using this technique, because the real page is only visible if your IP address is the same as (for example) a search engine's spider.

■ IRC

Internet Relay Chat. An Internet service accessed through software programs that features real-time communication on channels devoted to specific topics.

■ ISO 9000

International Organisation for Standardisation's series of international standards for information systems intended for compatibility and quality assurance. These are intended to foster world trade. ISO 9000 Translated into Plain English http://www.connect-.ab.ca/~praxiom/.

ISO standards include:

ISO 9001- 'Quality Systems - Model for Quality Assurance in Design, Development, Production, Installation and Servicing',

ISO 9002 - 'Model for Quality Assurance in Production, Installation and Servicing',

ISO 9003 - 'Model for Quality Assurance in Final Inspection and Test.',

ISO 9004 - a document guide to further quality development,

ISO 14000 - a new standard to address environmental issues.

Most importantly, ISO is comprised of many other standard setting bodies, including the following:

ANSI (American National Standards Institute)

ITU (International Telecommunication Union)

IEEE (Institute of Electrical and Electronic Engineers)

VESA (Video Electronics Standards Association)

The key to these standards has been an audit and certification system. Companies seeking ISO certification must have an audit. The certification has become important, especially in Europe, for market advantages, cost reduction, access to markets, improved communications, reduced political conflicts, documentation and dissemination processes and employee training. Many of the standards are focused upon meeting paperwork and record keeping requirements.

ISO 9660

the data-format and file-naming conventions that ensure CD-based data can be accessed across multiple computer platforms.

ITAD

Integrated Telephone Answering Device that avoids tape recording by using direct digital recorders for telephones.

IXC

Inter eXchange Carrier. Another name for a long distance telephone company. See **LEC**.

jack in

to log in to a machine or connect to a network. Derived from cyberpunk fiction.

Java

Java is a network-friendly programming language invented by Sun Microsystems.

Java is often used to build large, complex systems that involve several different computers interacting across networks, for example transaction processing systems.

Java is also becoming popular for creating programs that run in small electronic devices, such as mobile telephones.

A very common use of Java is to create programs that can be safely downloaded to your computer through the Internet and immediately run without fear of viruses or other harm to your computer or files. Using small Java programs (called *'Applets'*), Web pages can include functions such as animations, calculators and other fancy tricks.

Java virtual machine

software that allows Java to run on different platforms (operating systems.)

JavaScript

JavaScript is a programming language that is mostly used in web pages, usually to add features that make the web page more interactive. When JavaScript is included in an *HTML* file it relies upon the browser to interpret the JavaScript. When JavaScript is combined with Cascading Style Sheets (CSS) and later versions of HTML (4.0 and later) the result is often called DHTML.

javastation

a low cost hardware unit that provides users an Internet browser specifically designed to employ Java.

JDBC

Java Database Connectivity standard that allows Java to interface with databases. See **database, IDL** and **Java**.

■ JDK

Java Development Kit. A software development package from Sun Microsystems that implements the basic set of tools needed to write, test and debug Java applications and applets.

■ jeeves

see **search engine**.

■ JITT

Just-In-Time Training. In many technical and complex areas it is not practical for employees or other persons to be knowledgeable about all details at all times. For example, it has become impractical for auditors to have a working knowledge of every accounting and auditing standard in the United States and other nations. Physicians and other medical practitioners cannot have instant recall of details of every disease and combination of medical symptoms and treatments. JITT refers to a process (that is usually aided by computers, compact discs, computer networks and/or teleconferencing) in which the person receives training 'just-in-time' when it is needed for a particular purpose. The JITT process may change the entire process of education and training, because the focus may become how to effectively access and utilise JITT rather than how to teach students and/or employees technical details that have to be memorised long before they are needed in practice.

■ Joint Photographic Experts Group (JPEG)

an image compression standard for still photographs that is commonly used on the web.

■ joy stick

a remote control device that can be used in place of a keyboard or a mouse to allow for interactions between a computer and its user. Joy sticks are commonly used for computer games and usually connect through a serial port.

■ jughead

searchable index software that can be applied to a an organis-ation's gopher menus similar to VERONICA. It supposedly was named for its inventor, Rhett Jones, as Jonzy's Universal Gopher Hierarchy Excavation and Display. But since the search tools archie and VERONICA came before it, the name obviously preceded the acronym. See **archie**.

■ jukeboxes

hardware devices for stacking discs, especially compact discs such as CD-ROM discs for a computer. Two hardware options for moving from one active CD to another are called jukeboxes and arrays. Jukeboxes typically take up only one SCSI device spot but they can be slow to access while the robot finds, extracts, moves and inserts each disc. Arrays are linked CD devices that are both faster and cheaper than jukeboxes.

■ k or k

number prefix meaning 1000 or in computer usage, the similar 2^{10}. In some conventions, k means 1000 and K means 2^{10}.

■ kaleida

this is a software/hardware development company (along with the PowerPC and another company called Taligent) funded in a joint venture by Apple Corporation and IBM. The first noteworthy product is the long-delayed ScriptX hypermedia package designed to cross multiple platforms.

■ kbps

kilobytes per second

■ Kerberos

Kerberos is a network authentication protocol. It is designed to provide strong authentication for client/server applications by using secret-key cryptography. A free implementation of this protocol is available from the Massachusetts Institute of Technology. Kerberos is available in many commercial products as well.

■ kermit

a common terminal emulation program and file transfer protocol that can be used across dialup and telnet connections. It is much slower than xmodem, ymodem and zmodem in most implementations, but it has the advantage of being able to transfer 8-bit files across a 7-bit telnet connection, which the others will not do. It was developed at Columbia U and is widely used in academia, probably because it is free. It was named for the frog.

■ key

information that causes a cipher to encrypt or decrypt information in a distinctive way. Individual keys are usually associated with individual entities or at most a pair of entities.

■ Key Distribution Centre (KDC)

a device that provides secret keys to allow pairs of hosts to encrypt traffic directly between themselves. This is the basis of the Kerberos system.

■ Key Encrypting Key (KEK)

crypto key used to encrypt session or data keys and never used to encrypt the data itself.

■ key escrow

mechanism for storing copies of crypto keys so that third parties can recover them if necessary to read information encrypted by others.

key recovery

mechanism for determining the key used to encrypt some data, possibly through the use of an escrowed key.

keyword

a word which forms (part of) a search engine query.

keyword density

a property of the text in a web page which indicates how close together the keywords appear. Some search engines use this property for Positioning. Analysers are available which allow comparisons between pages. Pages can then be produced with the similar keyword densities to those found in high-ranking pages.

keyword domain name

the use of keywords as part of the URL to a website. Positioning is improved on some search engines when keywords are reinforced in the URL.

keyword phrase

a phrase which forms (part of) a search engine query.

keyword purchasing

the buying of search keywords from search engines, usually to control banner ad placement. All the major search engines insist that keyword purchasing is only used for banner ad placement and doesn't influence search results. The display of banner ads for bought keywords can be studied using a service called Bannerstake from Thomson and Thomson, which returns the banner ads displayed when particular queries are used.

keyword stuffing

the repeating of keywords and keyword phrases in META tags or elsewhere.

keyword(s)

a word searched for in a search command. Keywords are searched in any order. Use spaces to separate keywords in simple keyword searching. To search keywords exactly as keyed (in the same order).

kill file

a file used by some USENET reading programs that filters out unwanted messages, usually from a particular author or on a particular subject. If you add someone to your kill file, you arrange for the person to be ignored by your newsreader.

kilobyte

a thousand bytes. Actually, usually 1024 (2^{10}) bytes.

kilohertz

unit of measure that equals a frequency of 1 thousand cycles per second. See also **hertz** and **megahertz**.

kiosk

a multimedia display system such as those used in marketing displays at conferences and in stores. Kiosks are typically used for demonstrations and may be self-contained hardware units having computer, video and audio capabilities.

kiss

keep It Simple Stupid refers mainly to the authoring of electronic books and/or development of software in which success often depends upon keeping the learning and usage mindlessly simple. See also **authoring**.

kluge

a quick fix to a problem that places expediency over elegance. Pronounced 'klooj'. Variant spelling is 'kludge'.

knowbie

a person who understands the finer details of computer networking. See also **hacker** and **newbie.**

knowbot

an artificially intelligent computer program that automates the search for animation.

lamer, lammer

a derogatory term for a wanna-be programmer or hacker or cracker who is clueless, often destructive and not as expert as he thinks he is a 'luser'.

LAN

Local Area Network. A network that depicts any computer network technology that operates at high speed over short distances (up to a few thousand metres). A LAN may refer to a network in a given department or within a given firm or campus. It differs from computer networks that cross wider geographic spaces such as those networks on a WAN network. A LAN does not use the public arteries of the Internet like intranets and VPNs.

LCD

Liquid Crystal Device computer/video panel and projector displays. Miniature television sets, laptop computers and notebook computers generally use some type of LCD display due to difficulties in manufacturing portable cathode ray tube monitors. LCD displays may come in black and white, grey scale and various degrees of colour depth. The panels that can be laid on top of overhead projectors for displaying computer images on walls and large screens are called 'LCD panels'. LCD panels differ as to whether they can display full-motion video as well as computer images.

LDAP

acronym for Lightweight Directory Access Protocol. It is a protocol for accessing information directories such as organisations, individuals, phone numbers and addresses. It is based on the X.500

directory protocols, but it is simpler and unlike X.500, it supports TCP/IP for Internet usage. The standards are specified in RFC 1777.

leased line

a permanently established connection between computers over a dedicated phone line which is leased from a telephone carrier.

least privilege

feature of a system in which operations are granted the fewest permissions possible in order to perform their tasks.

LEC

Local Exchange Carrier. The local telephone company serving an area. There are Incumbent LECs (ILEC)—those with a local monopoly—and Competitive LECs (CLEC). Long distance companies, also known as IXCs (Inter Exchange Carriers), pay LECs a fee for access to local telephones.

leet

short for elite. Jargon used by hackers and crackers to refer to themselves or to the sites they frequent to share pirated software and information.

legacy

an adjective that refers to technology associated with old corporate programs, such as those on mainframes. Increasingly used as a put-down, the opposite of cutting edge.

lightweight crypto

set of crypto capabilities that is as strong as possible but still sufficiently weak to qualify for favourable treatment under U. S. export regulations.

limiting to a field

requiring that a keyword or phrase appear in a specific field of documents retrieved. Most often used to limit to the 'Title' field in order to find documents primarily about one or more keywords. (Can be used for other fields).

line noise

static over a telephone line that interferes with network communications.

link

a highlighted word or picture within a hypertext document that when clicked bring you to another place within the document or to another document altogether.

link 'rot'

term used to describe the frustrating and frequent problem caused by the constant changing in URLs. A Web page or search tool offers a link and when you click on it, you get an error message (e.g., 'not available') or a page saying the site has moved to a new URL. Search engine spiders cannot keep up with the changes. URLs change frequently because the documents are moved to new computers, the file structure on the computer is reorganised or sites are discontinued. If there is no referring link to the new URL, there is little you can do but try to search for the same or an equivalent site from scratch.

■ link encryption

crypto services applied to data as it travels on data links.

■ link popularity

see **page popularity.**

■ links

these are the hypertext connections between Web pages. This is a synonym for hotlinks or hyperlinks.

■ Linux

a widely used Open Source Unix-like operating system. Linux was first released by its inventor Linus Torvalds in 1991. There are versions of Linux for almost every available type of computer hardware from desktop machines to IBM mainframes. The inner workings of Linux are open and available for anyone to examine and change as long as they make their changes available to the public. This has resulted in thousands of people working on various aspects of Linux and adaptation of Linux for a huge variety of purposes, from servers to TV-recording boxes.

■ list server

an automated mailing list distribution system. List servers maintain a list of e-mail addresses to be used for mass e-mailing. Subscribing and unsubscribing to the list is accomplished by sending a properly formatted e-mail message to the list server.

■ listproc

one of the common types of E-mail discussion lists.

■ live

when used in reference to a World Wide Web file, this term designates an object linked to another layer of information.

■ log file

a file maintained on a server in which details of all file accesses are stored. Analysing log files can be a powerful way to find out about a web site's visitors, where they come from and which queries are used to access a site. Various software packages are available to analyse log files and some are listed below.

■ login

1. the account name used to gain access to a computer system. Not a secret (contrast with *Password*).
2. the act of connecting to a computer system by giving your credentials (usually your 'username' and 'password.)

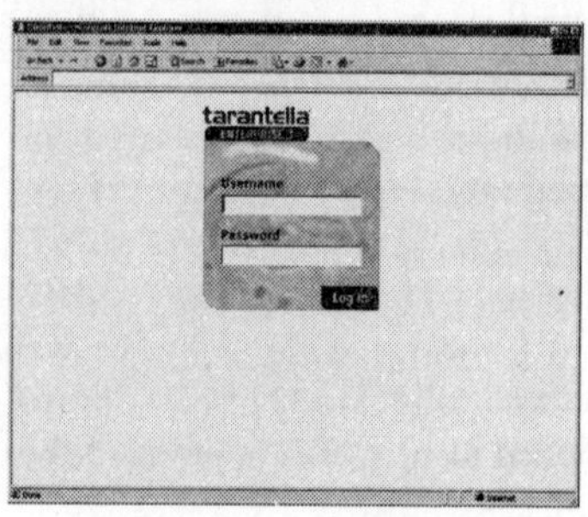

■ LOL

abbreviation for 'Laughing Out Loud'.

■ looksmart

a medium-sized directory. The URL is http://www.looksmart.com.

■ loop

a programming technique of creating a series of repeating actions. Usually, there is some event specified as part of the loop, which triggers the ending of the repetitious action.

■ lossy

a term coined by graphics programmers to refer to a technique of shrinking file sizes by giving away some precision of detail. JPEG is the most common of these. By reducing the so-called quality of a picture when you save it, you can make the file size smaller. Many pictures can take a lot of loss of fine detail before it becomes noticeable on a web page.

■ Lotus Notes

a networking set of application programs from Lotus Development Corporation, now owned by IBM Corporation, which allows organisations to share documents, databases and exchange electronic mail messages. Purportedly, Lotus Notes was the major reason why Lotus was purchased by IBM Corporation. An interactive web server called Domino was introduced in 1996 so that Lotus Notes users could build intranets on the Internet.

■ low risk application

computer applications that, if penetrated or disrupted, would not cause a serious loss for an enterprise.

■ lurk

listening in to a mailing list, message base, chat room or newsgroup without participating. Newcomers are encouraged to lurk for a while as they get the feel of things. The term 'lurker' is sometimes used negatively to refer to people who take from discussions, but never give.

■ luser

a user who is a loser. The result of a dispute at MIT some years ago where computer error messages referred to errors by users. Others changed users to losers and the dispute continued until someone coined the term lusers, which everyone liked.

■ lycos

one of the largest search engines, Lycos appears to be moving towards becoming a directory and is using the Open Directory for some search results. It can be slow to index new sites. The lycos spider ignores meta tags in pages. Lycos can be found at http://www.lycos.com.

■ lynx

a text-only web browser that was an early workhorse before the web gained its graphical face. It is still used extensively today by the visually impaired, people with limited systems and those with slow connections who don't want to take the time to load graphics.

m

number prefix, short for mega.

mac

an abbreviation of the popular Macintosh computers manufactured and sold by Apple Corporation. These computers contain what is called the Macintosh Operating System that will only run software written for that processor.

MAC address

Media Access Control address, given to a device in a network. It consists of a 48-bit hexadecimal number (12 characters). The address is normally assigned to a device, such as a network card, when it is manufactured.

machine

commonly used for 'computer'.

machine language

a program in the form of a series of binary codes that are understandable by the CPU. 99.9% of the time programmers write their code in another 'higher level' programming language, which in turn translates their code into machine language.

macro virus

a virus contained in and spread by a macro language program that supplements a word processed document or spread sheet. These are by far the most common type of viruses now and they can easily be spread in attachments to e-mail. Never open an e-mail attachment without running anti-virus software first. If you need recommendations for good anti-virus software, ask in the Navigating the Net Message Board.

MAE

Metropolitan Area Exchange or Metropolitan Area Ethernet. A major Internet Network Access Point (NAP) where different providers and networks hand off traffic to each other. The two main MAEs in the United States are MAE East in Washington, DC and MAE West in Silicon Valley.

mailbomb

the act of sending massive amounts of e-mail to a single address with the malicious intent of disrupting the system of the recipient. Mailbombing is considered a serious breach of Netiquette and is probably illegal.

mailbomb

flood a single e-mail address with a high volume of mail. Used to retaliate against an individual or organisation that has bothered the sender(s) in some way. Please note that the practice violates all ISP user agreements and wastes bandwidth and resources. Its effects go far beyond the annoyance to the addressee. Don't try it!

mailing list

a discussion group that occurs via mass e-mail distributions. Mailing lists are usually maintained by individuals utilising list server software. List servers maintain a list of e-mail addresses to be used for the mailing list. Subscribing and unsubscribing to the list is accomplished by sending a properly formatted e-mail message to the list server. There are two types of mailing lists: moderated and unmoderated. To send a message to an unmoderated list, you e-mail it to the list server, which automatically e-mails your message to every name on the list. To send a message to a moderated list, you e-mail it to the mailing list's moderator who would then send it on to the list server for distribution.

mainframe

a high-level computer designed for intensive computational tasks and used by large corporations. Mainframes are often shared by multiple users connected to the computer via terminals. Originally refers to the cabinet containing the CPU of a room-sized batch-processing machine.

majordomo

one of the common types of E-mail discussion lists.

malibu graphics chip

see **kaleida**.

Man In Middle (MIM)

attack against public key exchange in which the attacker substitutes their own public key for the requested public key. Also called a bucket brigade attack.

mandatory protection

security mechanism in a computer that unconditionally blocks particular types of activities. For example, most multi-user systems have a 'user mode' that unconditionally blocks users from directly accessing shared peripherals. In networking applications, a small number of vendors use mandatory protection to prevent attacks on Internet servers from penetrating other portions of the host system.

MAPI

Message Application Programming Interface. A standard Windows interface for messaging that enables different mail programs and other mail-aware applications like word processors and spreadsheets to exchange messages and attachments with each other.

masquerade

attack in which an entity takes on the identity of a different entity without authorisation.

matlab

two important features of MATLAB software are the integration of MATLAB with Microsoft's Word for Windows and the Symbolic Math Toolbox for advanced visualisations of mathematical functions.

■ matrix

a superset of the Internet that includes all networks and computers that can exchange e-mail.

■ mbps

abbreviation for megabytes per second.

■ MCF

see **RDF**.

■ MCI

Media Control Interface established by Microsoft Corporation that has become a popular standard for Windows authors and users. MCI menus drop down to let users select input sources such as CD-Audio inputs, videodisc inputs, MIDI sequencers and auxiliary sources such as inputs from a stereo set or a videotape player. These standards also mean that certain types of files should play on MCI systems (e.g., WAV files should play audio and AVI files should play video on MCI systems). It is recommended that any hardware/software purchased for the PC go beyond MCI standards and be Sound Blaster compatible. This does not mean that you must buy multimedia upgrades from Creative Labs. It only means that your system is compatible with the popular standard established by Sound Blaster. Also, a standard control interface for multimedia devices and media files, including a command-message interface and a command-string interface.

■ MD

see **minidisc.**

■ MDA

Model Driven Architecture in information systems (rather than management's discussion and analysis MDA in financial reporting). Model-Driven Architecture or MDA, embodies the conundrum: Is the glass half full or is it half empty? Even though the MDA standard is still evolving, many products claim to be compliant with it and early adopters are developing apps with them.

MDA vendors claim that today's products can generate between 40% and 80% of the completed code for a given app based on models created with UML and customers and analysts back up those claims. MDA's purported benefits go beyond automatic code generation and the reduction of development costs, but those advantages are longer-term and most have yet to be proven outside of theoretical conversations. They include factors like eventual code and model reuse and more effective fulfilment of user requirements. One advantage touted by the MDA camp is the ability to swap out underlying technologies — OSs or languages, for example — by simply revamping the platform-specific model and then regenerating the applications.

Still, a split remains between current users of these products — mostly architects who speak UML or another modelling language —

and the targeted group of developers who believe they can do a better job of writing apps than any code generator. And it is developers that need to be convinced that these tools can make their work lives more meaningful by allowing them to concentrate on the creative stuff.

■ media streaming

see **web streaming**.

■ medium risk application

computer application in which a disruption or other security problem could cause losses to the enterprise and some such losses are an acceptable cost of doing business.

■ medium strength crypto

set of crypto capabilities that may qualify for favourable export treatment by the U. S. government if the vendor is actively developing crypto products that contain key escrow features. The typical medium strength algorithm is DES with 56 bit keys.

■ mega

prefix meaning one million (10^6) or in computer usage, the similar value 1,048,576 (2^{20}).

■ megabyte

a million *bytes*. Actually, technically, 1024 kilobytes.

■ megahertz

unit of measure that equals a frequency of 1 million cycles per second. See also **hertz** and **kilohertz**

■ meltdown

a state of complete network overload that grinds all traffic to a halt.

■ menu

a list of options, each of which performs a desired action such as choosing a command or applying a particular format to a part of a document. Menus are commonly used in graphical interfaces.

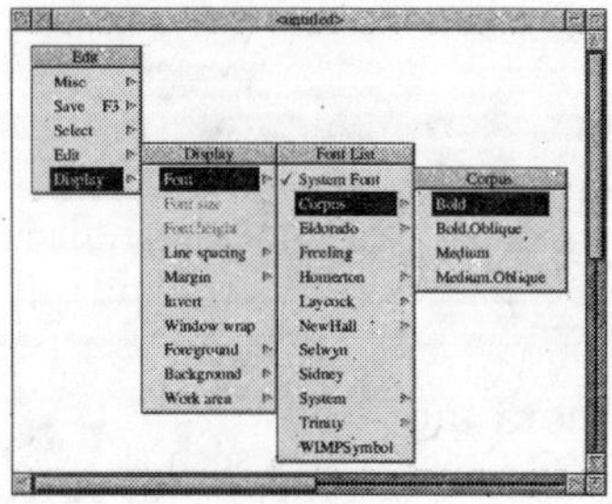

■ message

information sent from one entity to another on the network. A single message may be divided into several packets for delivery to the destination and then reassembled by the receiving host.

■ message header

the information at the beginning of an e-mail or bulletin board message. Message headers contain the identities of the author and recipients, the subject of the message and the date the message was sent.

■ Message Security Protocol (MSP)

e-mail crypto protocol developed as part of the SDNS program and being used in the Defence Message System.

■ meta search

a search of searches. A query is submitted to more than one search engine or directory and results are reported from all the engines, possibly after removal of duplicates and sorting.

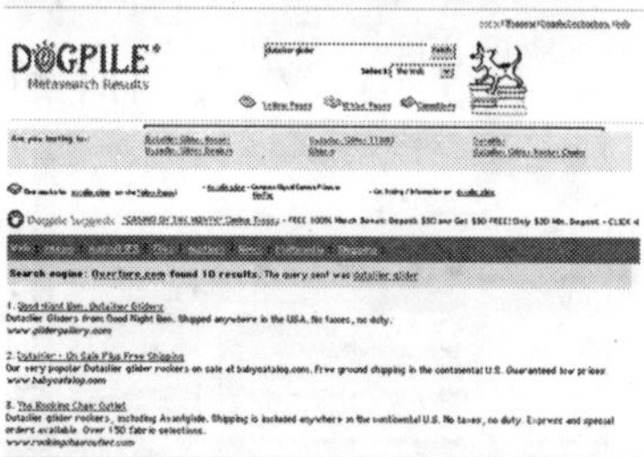

■ meta tag

a specific kind of HTML tag that contains information not normally displayed to the user. Meta tags contain information about the page itself, hence the name ('meta' means 'about this subject'). Typical uses of Meta tags are to include information for search engines to help them better categorise a page.

■ metacrawler

a meta search engine found at http://www.metacrawler.com. Results from various search engines are summarised in an easy to read form.

■ metadata

information about data or more specifically, the descriptive information provided in meta tags in an HTML or XML document header about that document. Active efforts are ongoing to propose standards for machine and human readable metadata to be used with web resources to aid in resource discovery.

■ metafile

a graphics format that combines the features of bitmap and vector graphics. Common types of metafile formats are CGM, Corel Draw CDR files, encapsulated Postscript EPS files, Adobe Illustrator, Word Perfect Graphics WPG files, PICT and RTF.

■ metafind

a meta search engine found at http://www.metafind.com.

■ meta-search engine

search engines that automatically submit your keyword search to several other search tools and retrieve results from all their databases. Convenient time-savers for relatively simple keyword searches (one or two keywords or phrases in ' ').

■ metaverse

this term describes a virtual online representation of reality.

■ mff

see **MIDI.**

■ mhz

see **megahertz.**

■ microsoft camcorder

see **video.**

■ **microsoft tiger video**

see **video server.**

■ **MID**

see **MIDI.**

■ **middleware**

second generation network computing applications extends data transfers from the client computers back to the web server and/or database server computers. Software for doing this is commonly termed 'middleware.' Software mediates between an application program on a server and a network of client machines. Middleware manages the interaction between applications across the heterogeneous computing platforms of client computers.

■ **MIDI**

Musical Instrument Digital Interface audio standardised hardware parameters set under MPC standards for MIDI interfaces that connect electronic keyboards, synthesisers and related devices to computers. Musicians may record music into computer (MIDI) files that require much less storage space than WAV files that contain complete files of digitised sounds. A MIDI file does not contain digitised sound. Instead, such a file contains the information needed to play such sounds from a MIDI-compatible device. Music files may be played back (somewhat analogous to the old player pianos) on the MIDI. MIDI sound files are generally of higher quality than their WAV audio files that play on computers without MIDI interfaces. The MIDI is extremely popular among composers and arrangers of music who want to utilise computer aids in their tasks. The mff and mid MIDI file formats are popular file extensions for MIDI files that will run on most PC computers.

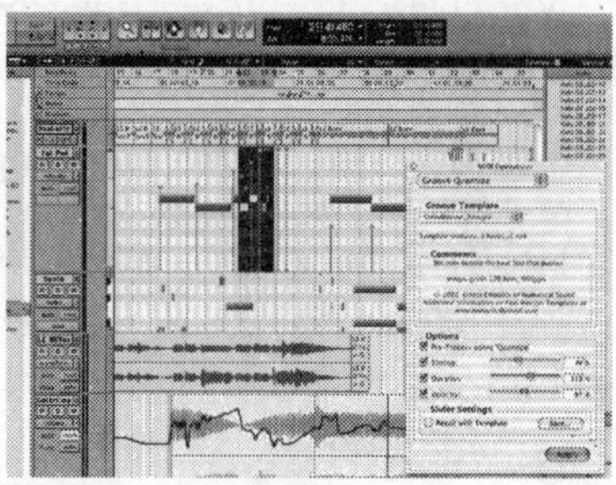

■ **millenium bug**

the set of problems occurring on January 1, 2000 and other related dates caused by short-sighted programming that coded the years with only 2 digits. Ambiguity arises in the year 2000 as to whether 00 represents the year 1900 or the year 2000 and calculations based on it may fail or produce incorrect results. It can affect software, hardware, operating systems and devices with embedded software. Another common programming error is failing to account for the year 2000 as a leap year (by the 400 year rule).

■ **MIME**

Multipurpose Internet Mail Extensions. The standard for attaching binary files to Internet mail messages. Its usage has been extended to identifying and handling file types encountered by web servers and browsers. Binary types include audio, video, graphics, spreadsheets, formatted word-processor documents, executable programs, etc. An e-mail program is said to be MIME Compliant if it can both send and receive files using MIME. When binary files are sent using the MIME standard they are converted (encoded) into text for mailing and then decoded by the receiving mailer. If the receiving mailer is not MIME compliant, the file is received in encoded form.

■ mimosa

see **video server.**

■ minidisc

it is used in a variety of contexts to depict miniature 'MD' optical discs and/or magnetic discs smaller than the standard 4.72 inch CD. Some MD alternatives such as the Sony MD Data 2.5 inch disk are smaller than floppy discs but hold nearly as much as a CD-ROM. The Sony version holds up to 74 minutes of CD quality audio or 140 Mb of data storage. The most typical MD

size is the 2.5 inch audio disc. The term MD-Data refers to a minidisc used to record computer files and hypermedia presentations.

■ mining company

a large directory spread over many different URLs The main URL is http://www.minin-gco.com.

■ MIPS

Million Instructions Per Second. Benchmark for rating computer processor CPU speed. Comparisons of MIPS ratings, however, can be misleading since the speed of access to peripheral equipment has become so important in overall computing performance.

■ mirror

generally speaking, 'to mirror' is to maintain an exact copy of something. Probably the most common use of the term on the Internet refers to 'mirror sites' which are *web* sites or FTP sites that maintain copies of material originated at another location, usually in order to provide more widespread access to the resource. For example, one site might create a library of software and 5 other sites might maintain mirrors of that library.

■ mission critical

indispensable. Usually describes applications such as databases or process control software that are deemed essential to a company's operation and that typically run on mainframes or workstation rather than on personal computers. A nuclear power plant's operator console software is mission critical.

■ **misspellings**

people quite often spell words incorrectly when using search engines. Pages, which use common misspellings will quite often receive extra hits, so it is a useful technique to include common misspellings of words in alt tags, keywords, page names and titles. A similar effect occurs when spaces are missed out and words are accidentally joined together.

■ **MMDS**

Multipoint Multichannel Distribution Service using neighbourhood line-of-sight microwave antennas to transmit wireless data from homes to Internet providers. Cable companies are employing this technology that will allow for fast wireless Internet connections to homes and businesses. See also **DSL** and **ISDN**.

■ **mode**

one of several ways to apply a block cipher to a data stream. Typical modes include CBC, CFB and OFB.

■ **modem**

a device that enables a computer to send and receive information over a telephone line. Internal modems are circuit cards that are plugged straight into the computer's motherboard. External modems are small electronic boxes attached to the serial port with a cable.

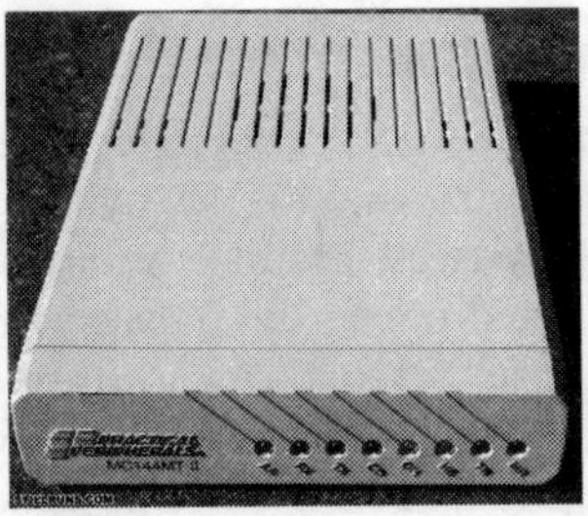

■ **modem mantra**

the sound a modem makes while connecting with another modem.

■ **moderator**

a person or small group of people who manage a mailing list or newsgroup. Moderators determine which messages can be seen by the entire group.

■ **mods**

hacker slang for modifications to hardware or software, especially bug fixes or minor design changes.

■ **modulus**

in public key crypto, this refers to part of the public key.

■ **MOO**

Mud Object-Oriented. See **MUD**.

■ **moof**

when you get disconnected from the Internet for no apparent reason, it's common to blame the Moof monster. For example, when returning to a chat after being unintentionally disconnected, you can tell your cyberbuddies, 'Sorry I left so suddenly, I got moofed!'

MORF?

abbreviation of 'Male or Female?'

morphing

process of special effects video and/or computer animation that distorts images in motion. What started out in the movies as perverse distortions and unreal 'morphed' images has gained respectability in science as a means of visualising data and dynamic changes in data. Originally, morphing was only something professionals could do on very expensive workstations. Now morphing software and hardware requirements are much more modest.

mosaic

the first WWW browser that was available for the Macintosh, Windows and UNIX all with the same interface. Mosaic really started the popularity of the Web. The source-code to Mosaic was licensed by several companies and used to create many other web browsers.

Mosaic was developed at the National Centre for Supercomputing Applications (NCSA), at the University of Urbana-Champange in Illinois, USA. The first version was released in late 1993.

motherboard

a circuit board or 'logic board' inside the computer that contains the central processing unit (CPU), microprocessor support chips, RAM and slots for adding expansion boards such as audio, scanner, SCSI and video boards. Multimedia chips such as DSP audio and video chips will increasingly be put on the motherboard rather than on expansion boards.

mozart

the name given to Apple's operating system 7.5 for Mac and PowerPC computers. New features include multitasking, improved networking, better multimedia support and DOS/Windows capabilities.

mp3

see **audio**.

MPC

a Multimedia PC refers to combinations of PC hardware that meet multimedia hardware-combination (e.g., audio and video boards for computers) standards set by the Multimedia Marketing Council to make multimedia hardware products of vendors more compatible. The MPC1 Level 1 standard requires a 386 PC with a minimum of 2 Mb of RAM. The MPC2 Level 2 standard requires a 486SX or greater PC with 4 Mb of RAM. A variety of PC manufacturers use the MPC trademark. Consumers can then be assured that MPC hardware from one vendor will be compatible with hardware of another vendor. Also, software written for MPC hardware should run on any MPC equipment. The term is generally used in conjunction with CD-ROM multimedia hardware. A CD-ROM player, for example, should run on a computer with an MPC trademark provided the player is MPC compatible. It is probably best not to invest in multimedia PC hardware that is not compatible with MPC standards. In the future, MPC standards will dwindle in importance as more and more vendors build audio and video hardware on the motherboard rather than as boards to place into expansion slots.

■ MPEG

Moving Pictures Experts Group. Systems boards and compression standards (e.g., MPEG-2 and MPEG-1) for the most popular emerging form of compressed full-motion video standard for computer file storage. MPEG compression requires MPEG playback boards and/or MPEG authoring boards such as the Optibase MPG-1000 digital video codec (compression/decompression) board (800-451-5101). Although MPEG-2 is superior to MPEG-1, MPEG-2 requires at least quad speed CD-ROMs that, thereby, limits the use of MPEG-2 in the commercial market. MPEG-2 works much better with CD-DVD.

■ MS-Windows

see **Windows**.

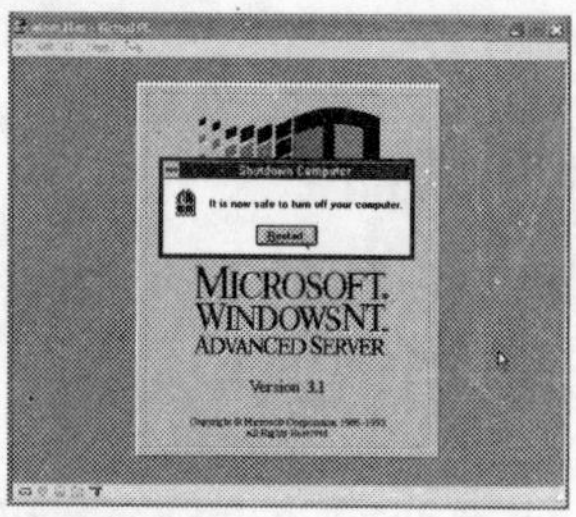

■ MTS/SAP

Multichannel Television Sound and Second Audio Program. Dbx system for compressing stereo audio in a technical fashion too complicated to explain here. See also **dbx**.

■ MUD

acronym for Multi-User Domain, Multi-User Dimension or Multi-User Dungeon. An online interactive computer game or exploration medium. Early MUDs were Dungeons & Dragons-like games in text-only forms, but they have grown into many other forms, too. They are now used for social gatherings, interactive learning, chat rooms and much more, as well as the old-style entertaining games. Originally accessible only through telnet, many of them have migrated to the web and even appeared in graphical virtual reality and 3D forms. Variations are known as MUSHes, MUSEs and MOOs.

■ Multicast Backbone (Mbone)

a high-speed network protocol used to broadcast audio and video over the Internet.

■ multicrawl

a parallel search engine which offers users their own branded versions.

■ multimedia

the ability to combine audio, visual and possibly other types of hardware into a presentation. For example, a 'multimedia' classroom will typically have projection hardware and switching controls that make it easy for teachers to switch back and forth between computer projections, videotape projections, audio CDs, 35mm slides, videodiscs, CD-I players, etc. Although hypermedia presentations may require multimedia facilities, the two terms are not synonymous.

■ multimedia upgrade

hardware additions (usually insert boards or plug-and-play devices) to computers that make some aspect of multimedia operational. The lowest form of upgrade is an audio upgrade kit. This is usually followed by a digital video upgrade kit. Other upgrades may include CD-ROM players, videodisc players, video scan converters, mixers, speakers, video editing systems, etc. Common upgrades meet MPC standards. See also **MPC** and **multimedia**.

■ multimedia video processor

a DSP multimedia processing chip from Texas Instruments that is claimed to be 20 to 50 times more powerful than Intel's Pentium according to a survey report. The MVP processor combines parallel-processing, DSP and RISC technology.

■ multiple domain names

the use of several extra domains to provide gateway pages or gateway sites to the main site.

■ multiple keyword tags

the use of more than one Keywords META tag in order to try to increase the relevancy of the best keywords on a page. This is not recommended. It may be detected as a spamming technique or all but one of the tags may simply be ignored.

■ multiple titles

it used to be possible to repeat the HTML title tag in the header section of a page several times to improve search engine positioning. Most search engines now detect this trick.

■ multiplexor

a complex piece of telephone equipment which combines the data stream of several leased lines for transmission over a single higher bandwidth leased line. Multiplexors are used in the construction of WANs.

■ multisession recording

creating a disk in several stages rather than all at once.

■ multitasking

execution of programs simultaneously on a single computer. In newer operating systems, two or more programs may be running 'in the background' while the user is concentrating on another program running 'in the foreground'. Limits on how many programs can be run at the same time depend more upon hardware capacities, especially RAM amounts. Most operating systems now have multitasking capabilities. Multitasking differs from multiloading in which RAM contains multiple programs that can only be run one at a time. See also **operating system.**

■ Multi-user Dungeon (MUD)

an online fantasy role-playing game environment that takes place in telnet sessions. MUDs occur in text mode.

■ munition

anything that is useful in warfare. Crypto systems are munitions according to U. S. law. This is the rationale behind export controls on crypto systems.

■ MUSE

Multi-User Simulated Environment. One kind of MUD - usually with little or no violence.

■ nanosecond

a measurement of time. There are 1,000,000,000 nanoseconds in a second.

■ NAP

Network Access Point. A point where networks and service providers hand off traffic to each other. NAPs are typically the points with the worst congestion problems. When you encounter slow responses and run a traceroute, you will usually see the slowest connections occur where one network hands off to another.

■ napster/gnutella

software for sharing files over the Internet.

■ nastygram

a disapproving or flaming piece of e-mail.

■ National Computer Security Centre (NCSC)

U. S. government organisation that evaluates computing equipment for high security applications.

■ National Institute of Standards and Technology (NIST)

agency of the U. S. government that establishes national standards.

■ National Security Agency (NSA)

agency of the U. S. government responsible for intercepting foreign communications for intelligence reasons and for developing crypto systems to protect U. S. government communications.

■ native

the availability of a software package written directly for an operating system as opposed to running in emulation under some type of translation process. Emulation usually runs slower and possibly less effectively than native versions.

For example, Word Perfect and Microsoft Word have native versions for both Power Mac and Windows Chicago operating systems. Most Windows and DOS programs must be run in emulation on PowerPCs such that the speed advantages of the PowerPC are virtually lost due to not being able to run in native form. Whether or not Windows Chicago is truly better than the IBM and Apple competition operating systems may be a moot point if there are over 40 million Windows users that have installed or soon will install Windows Chicago. Market share determines the number of native software applications being developed for operating systems. Mac, UNIX and other operating systems are losing the native software development war to Windows Chicago and Windows 2000. Windows Chicago is almost certain to become the PC operating system standard of choice until its upgrade called Windows Cairo rolls off the line and/or Windows 2000 with upgraded object-oriented programming features become the operating systems of choice among users having newer hardware speed and memory components. See also **operating system**.

■ navigation

the navigation of a reader or user through learning and entertainment materials such as electronic books, courseware and networks.

■ navigator

a web browser application from Netscape.

■ NC

Network Computer. Oracle Corp. popularised this term for a simple device connected to the Internet that can do many tasks associated with PCs, but for a fraction of the cost.

■ nesting

a term used in Boolean searching to indicate the sequence in which operations are to be performed. Enclosing words in parentheses identifies a group or 'nest'. Groups can be within other groups. The operations will be performed from the innermost nest to the outmost and then from left to right.

■ net god

an individual who has achieved an exulted status due to notable technical accomplishments. This accolade is most frequently applied to those who have played a role in creating and developing USENET or the Internet.

■ net lingo

the slang commonly used on the Internet.

■ net surfing

browsing or exploring a network or the World Wide Web to find places of interest, usually without a specific goal in mind. Analogous to channel surfing with a TV remote control.

■ **net.police**

those who feel it's their appointed role to flame perceived violations of Netiquette.

■ **netbios**

a network communication protocol that NetWare can emulate.

■ **netiquette**

network etiquette or the set of informal rules of behaviour that have evolved in Cyberspace, including the Internet and online services.

■ **netizen**

derived from the term citizen, referring to a citizen of the Internet or someone who uses networked resources. The term connotes civic responsibility and participation.

■ **netlag**

a condition that occurs on the Internet in which response time is greatly slowed due to heavy traffic.

■ **netnews**

the content of USENET.

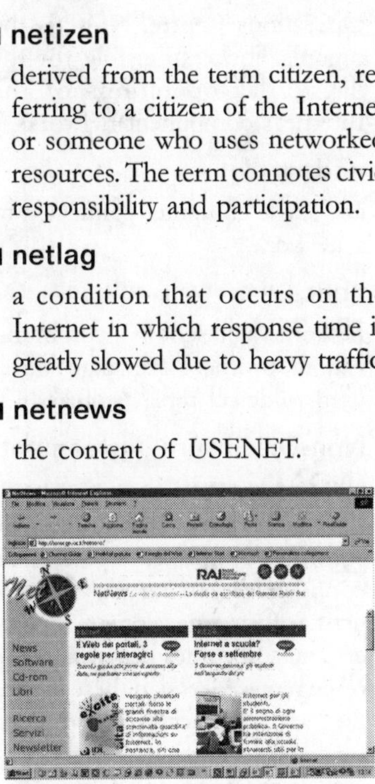

■ **netscape**

a WWW Browser and the name of a company. The Netscape browser was originally based on the Mosaic program developed at the National Centre for Supercomputing Applications (NCSA).

■ **netware**

a network operating system produced by Novell Incorporated.

■ **network**

any time you connect two or more computers together so that they can share resources, you have a computer network. Connect two or more networks together and you have an Internet.

■ **network address**

a hexadecimal number used to identify a network cabling system.

■ **network encryption**

crypto services applied to information above the data link level but below the application software level. This allows crypto protections to use existing networking services and existing application software transparently.

■ **newbie**

slang for someone who is new to the Internet or a specific aspect of it.

■ newsgroup

a public place where messages are posted for public consumption and response. The most available distribution of newsgroups is USENET, which contains over ten thousand unique newsgroups covering practically every human proclivity. The names of newsgroups are comprised of a string of words separated by periods.

■ NEXGEN

Next Generation microprocessor RISC chip from Alaris (a venture company formed with seed money from other famous companies) that was independently designed from Intel chips but is aimed at being equal to or better than the best Pentium alternatives from Intel.

■ NFS

Network File System, NFS is a protocol suite developed and licensed by Sun Microsystems that allows different makes of computers running different operating systems to share files and disk storage.

■ NIC

acronym for Network Interface Card, for example, an ethernet card in a network.

■ nintendo/sgi media cartridges

refer to data storage cartridges that are much faster than present CD-ROM alternatives for storing computer games, audio and video files.

■ NNTP - (Network News Transport Protocol)

the protocol used by client and server software to carry USENET postings back and forth over a TCP/IP network. If you are using any of the more common software such as *Netscape*, Nuntius, Internet Explorer, etc. to participate in newsgroups then you are benefiting from an NNTP connection.

■ NOC

the abbreviation for Network Operations Centre. NOC is the organisation responsible for the day-to-day operations of the Internet's component networks.

■ node

any single computer connected to a network.

■ nonce

random value sent in a communications protocol exchange, often used to detect replay attacks.

■ Non-Disclosure Agreement (NDA)

a contract commonly used by computer companies to protect the confidentiality of unreleased products. Software developers, reporters and sometimes beta testers are often required to sign these before they are given access to either information about upcoming products or the product itself.

■ northern light

a search engine with an additional 'pay to access' special collection of business, health and consumer publication articles. The first search engine to ban meta search engines from its database.

notebook computer

a portable computer about the size of a standard ring binder notebook. Original laptop computers were about the size of a briefcase. Notebook computers later emerged that could be carried inside a briefcase. Next, sub-notebook computers were introduced that could be carried inside a suit pocket, although the most popular models presently are notebook size portables. Multimedia versions are slightly larger and heavier. Although notebook computers do not have expansion slots for hardware modifications, SCSI, Ethernet, ISBN, video capture and other hardware options are available on PCMCI cards. Also, docking stations allow notebook computers to have most of the features of desktop computers, including expansion slots.

novell

a company based in Provo, Utah, that produces the NetWare network operating system.

NPTN

National Public Telecommunication Network in Cleveland that is dedicated to making communication, bulletin boards and networking services freely available through linkages of privately funded sources. See also **freenets**.

NREN

National Research and Education Network. In December 1991, the U.S. Congress passed the High Performance Computing and Communications Program. This will expand international networking to thousands of times its present capacities and uses. Although intended primarily for research and education, the NREN will carry commercial traffic in research and education in addition to the types of non-commercial traffic carried presently on the Internet. The NSFNet is now referred to as the 'Interim NREN'. See also **Internet**.

NSFNET

National Science Foundation Network. One of the Internet's primary backbone networks.

nslookup

a common Internet utility like ping and traceroute. Given an IP address or a DNS address, it will look up and show the corresponding DNS or IP address. There are nslookup utility programs available for every operating system, which you can use with a PPP or networked or shell account. The commonly used FTP program WS_FTP Pro includes a number of utilities including nslookup.

But if you have none of those readily available, there are other ways to do the same thing. If you are using Windows 95 or later, there is a traceroute utility built into the operating system. Select Start/ Run and type' command'. In the window that opens, type 'tracert address' without quotes and substituting the IP or DNS address you want to look up for 'address'. It will trace the path to the address, showing all intermediate addresses on the current path and the IP and DNS addresses for each. More simply, you can type 'nslookup address'.

Still another utility that will give you the information is WHOIS.

■ NSP

Native Signal Processing. Software from Intel that improves multimedia playback.

■ NTSC

National Television Standards Committee. Standards adopted in the 1960s by most nations in the Western Hemisphere, Japan and other parts of Asia. These standards differ from PAL and SECAM standards in other parts of the world. For example, videotapes recorded under NTSC standards will play on videotape players sold in the United States and Canada. NTSC videotapes will not, however, play in European countries, which have not adopted the NTSC standards.

■ nuke

to intentionally delete the entire contents of a given directory, hard drive or storage volume.

■ nysernet

an Internet network that links rural libraries with a high speed communications network. This network is a non-profit, equal-access network that has strong backing from major computer vendors and publishing firms.

■ object-oriented database systems

object-oriented database systems are quite different from the extremely relational database systems (e.g., MS Access, FoxPro, DBase, etc) that are extremely popular today.

■ objects

in programming terminology, a freestanding chunk of code that defines the properties of some thing. For example, a Net dictionary applet is an object that contains button objects, scrolling list objects, window objects, URL objects, definition objects, etc. Not all programming languages use this object model, the ones that do are said to be object-oriented.

■ OCR

Optical Character Recognition. Software and hardware used to Interpret scanned symbols into characters of text or numbers recognised as something other than mere graphics images.

■ ODBC

Open Database Connectivity refers to a standard for accessing different database systems in Visual Basic and Visual C++. Applications in most any software (e.g., Asymetrix ToolBook) can submit statements to ODBC using the ODBC type of SQL. ODBC then translates the code for use in common database systems such as Access, Paradox, dBase, Text, Excel and Btrieve databases. ODBC is based on Call-Level Interface and was defined by the SQL Access Group. Microsoft was one member of the group and was the first company to release a commercial product based on its work (under Microsoft Windows) but ODBC is not a Microsoft generated standard. ODBC drivers and development tools are available now for Microsoft Windows, Unix, OS/2 and Macintosh.

■ offline

1. as an adjective, not connected to a computer network.
2. as an adverb, not here or not now, as in 'Let's take this discussion offline'. Often used to indicate that a topic should be discussed privately rather than in a public forum.

■ OKI

Open Knowledge Initiative

■ OLAP

Online Analytical Processing. Database design in which data can be analysed from a multidimensional point of view. Whereas a relational database can be thought of as two-dimensional, a multidimensional database considers each data attribute (such as product, geographic sales region and time period) as a separate 'dimension'. OLAP software can locate the intersection of dimensions (all products sold in the Eastern region above a certain price during a certain time period) and display them. Attributes such as time periods can be broken down into sub-attributes.

■ OLE

Object Linking and Embedding. Standards established by Microsoft Corporation for Mac and Windows operating systems. In 1997, Microsoft declared that OLE no longer stands for object linking and embedding. Before 1997, however, OLE standards allowed the creation of links between documents and the embedding of documents in multiple applications. The OLE standards are designed to be 'dynamic' in that as changes are made in an object in one document, the changes are simultaneously made automatically in all linked documents. For example, in pasting from the clipboard, authors choose the Paste Link or Paste Special command rather than the Paste command in the Edit menu. Pasting in this way creates a dynamic link between the source document and the destination document. OLE also supports embedding which embeds the source document (or a portion of the document) into the destination file such that the two documents become a 'compound' file. Embedding is often used where a server file (creating embedded items) and client files (receiving embedded files) are in the system. In contrast to OLE linkages, OLE embedding edits in client files will not alter server files. This is not the case with OLE linkages, where any changes in a linked file will change all other linked files. Most word processor and spreadsheet software options have OLE capabilities.

■ **OLR**

Offline Reader. Software, which will collect messages for you from mail, newsgroups and message bases, send new ones you have written and let you read and respond offline.

■ **OLTP**

On-Line Transaction Processing in database management systems. See **database**.

■ **one time pad**

vernam cipher in which one bit of new, purely random key is used for every bit of data being encrypted.

■ **one time password**

password that can only be used once, usually produced by special password generating software or by a hardware token.

■ **one way hash**

hash function for which it is extremely difficult to construct two blocks of data that yield exactly the same hash result. Ideally, it should require a brute force search to find two data blocks that yield the same result.

■ **online**

1. currently connected to a host, opposite of offline.
2. referring to anything connected to a computer network.

■ **on-the-fly recording**

sending data from your hard disk directly to the CD-R burner, without creating a physical image file first. See also **CD-R**.

■ **OOP**

Object Oriented Programming.

■ **open**

a public standard in computer contexts that is the opposite of 'proprietary'. Open refers to software and hardware made from published specifications that anyone can copy — so customers have choice among multiple suppliers that compete on price and innovation.

■ **open content**

copyrighted information (such as this Glossary) that is made available by the copyright owner to the general public under license terms that allow reuse of the material, often with the requirement (as with this Glossary) that the re-user grant the public the same rights to the

modified version that the re-user received from the copyright owner.
Information that is in the Public Domain might also be considered a form of Open Content.

■ open directory project

a directory project run by thousands of volunteer editors. In principal, this is a very exciting and powerful way to organise the web. In practice, there have been some problems with the behaviour of some of the editors, which has caused some initial difficulty for the organisers. Initially known as NewHoo, the project is now part of Netscape (and therefore of AOL).

■ open source software

it is software for which the underlying programming code is available to the users so that they may read it, make changes to it and build new versions of the software incorporating their changes. There are many types of Open Source Software, mainly differing in the licensing term under which (altered) copies of the source code may (or must be) redistributed.

■ operating system

the master control software system that serves as a foundation for applications software. Examples of past, present and forthcoming operating systems include MS-DOS, Amiga DOS, Windows, Windows XP, Windows 2000, Windows Chicago, Windows Cairo, OS/2, Workplace OS, Apple/Mac Systems 7 and 8, NEXTStep, Rhapsody, Unix, SCO, AIX, HP/UX, HP/MPE, SCO Open Desktop, Solaris and UnixWARE (Novell). A second class of operating systems is known as real time processing. These are used more for on-the-fly control systems such as aviation control systems and military applications. Examples include the Intel Multibus and iRMX operating systems. For a comparative analysis of the 32-bit options, see PC/Computing Special Report (1994) where it is concluded that there are advantages and drawbacks of each option and no clear optimal choice at this juncture in time. For 10 years, Apple Corporation would not license its proprietary Mac operating system to other manufacturers.

■ optical drive

any medium or device using a laser beam for accessing data stored on an optical disc. Typical optical drives are CD drives and videodisc drives. However, there are many types of optical drives including those that can be written on and re-written on much like floppy discs or computer tape. To date, most optical drives have slower access time than magnetic drives. See also **CD** and **videodisc**.

■ optical scanner

see **OCR**.

optimisation

changes made to a web page to improve the positioning of that page with one or more search engines. A means of helping potential customers or visitors to find a web site. Optimisation may involve design/layout changes, new text for the title-tags, meta-tags, alt-attributes, headings and changes to the first 200-250 words of the main text. A large image map at the top of a page should be moved further down the page. Frames should be avoided (unless navigational links are also provided within the frames).

orthogonal

in mathematics, relating to or composed of right angles. Generalised to mean independent of, separate from or irrelevant to. For example, a message about the weather in Nebraska might be orthogonal to a discussion of the Java programming language.

Orthogonal Frequency Division Multiplexing (OFDM)

a multiplexing technique used in 802.11a WLANs, this technique minimises the effect of multipath distortion encountered in 802.11b networks.

OS/2

Operating System 2 introduced by IBM Corporation in 1992 and upgraded to OS/2 Warp in 1994. This is the first 32-bit processing system designed for PCs. It beat its rival Microsoft Windows 2000 to the market by almost two years. In early 1994, neither Windows 2000 nor OS/2 have made a huge dent in the DOS and Windows market. For example, there were only four million OS/2 adopters and 250,000 Windows 2000 adopters at the end of 1993 in comparison with over 40 million Microsoft Windows adopters. As older PCs are replaced by higher speed PCs with more memory, 32-bit processors will become more popular. OS/2 gets some high praises when compared with current 32-bit alternatives in PC/Computing Special Report (1994). At issue is whether OS/2 or Windows 2000 or Pink or some other operating system will saturate the market (after DOS, Windows, Apple/Mac and Windows Chicago stubbornly fade from the scene). OS/2 is a very reliable operating system that requires less PC capacity than Windows 2000. However, Windows 2000 has more networking utilities that may give it the competitive edge in the future. Until software vendors offer a wider array of options for either OS/2 or Windows 2000, the operating systems most widely used worldwide will continue to be DOS, Windows and Windows Chicago. An alternate IBM operating system called Workplace OS combines the object-oriented Workplace with the OS/2 operating environment. Since OS/2 Warp has such a small market, developers are not generating significant native software applications that run more efficiently in OS/2 vis-a-vis Windows. OS/2 Warp performance is evaluated and a forecast is made that IBM will abandon OS/2. Although OS/2 Warp runs DOS applications better than MS-DOS itself, it is very slow when trying to run Windows applications. Neither Apple Corporation nor IBM Corporation has been able to significantly gain market share against Microsoft Windows.

■ OSI

Open Systems Interconnect. This is a model for connecting computers together in a network. The model consists of seven distinct and separate layers of protocols.
Physical or Data Transport Layer. This most basic layer moves data over cables based on the physical address of each Network Interface Card (NIC). The most common types are Ethernet and token ring. Ethernet terminals and server (if present) are connected by a hub.
Data Link Layer. This layer frames the packets of data that are sent through the network with a header and a footer that include CRC data for error checking. PPP, frame relay and X.25 operate at this layer. Bridges connect local networks of the same type at this layer.
Network or Internet Protocol Layer. This layer puts an Internet Protocol wrapper around the data with source and destination addresses and sequencing information in its header. Routers, which connect networks of different types together, operate at this layer.
Transport Layer. This layer governs the setting of suitable packet sizes, segmenting and reassembling data, detecting errors and flow control. Packets are often received out of order and with errors. At this level, packets are sequenced correctly and requests for error free packets are transmitted until error-free packets have all been received.
Session Layer. This layer polices the communications between sender and destination. Only one end can speak at a time. It executes transactions like saving a file. If something interrupts the save, the session layer returns the action to its previous state, preventing corruption of data and the transaction can be attempted again.
Presentation Layer. This layer provides a standard interface between the network and application layers, allowing a wide variety of applications to exist.
Application Layer. This layer provides for standard interfaces for such functions as message handling and file transfer and remote login. It allows, for example, for different e-mail programs to be used, as long as they conform to the standard application layer interface. If you send a message constructed in VMSMAIL on a VAX system, it can be read by Eudora on a Windows system as long as the standard application interface for message handling is followed by both programs.

TCP/IP differs from the OSI model in that it combines the session, presentation and application layers into a single application layer.

■ OSI model

the Open Systems Interconnection (OSI) reference model for describing network protocols was devised by the Internet Standards Organisation. It divides protocols into seven layers to standardise and simplify definitions.

■ OTM

see **CORBA**

■ OTOH

chat acronym for 'On The Other Hand'.

■ outbox

a folder where you store mail before it about to be sent.

■ outernets

systems of computer networks that are not bundled on the Internet but nevertheless can be accessed to the Internet through gateways that translate outernet protocols into Internet protocols. The worldwide system of gateways is called the 'Matrix' or 'the Net'.

■ Output Feedback (OFB)

block cipher mode in which the cipher is used to generate the key stream. Also called autokey mode.

■ owl

Ontology Web Language (OWL) The OWL Web Ontology Language is designed for use by applications that need to process the content of information instead of just presenting information to humans. OWL facilitates greater machine interpretability of Web content than that supported by XML, RDF and RDF Schema (RDF-S) by providing additional vocabulary along with a formal semantics. OWL has three increasingly . expressive sublanguages: OWL Lite, OWL DL and OWL Full.

■ packet

a unit of data sent across a network. When a large block of data is to be sent over a network, it is broken up into several packets, sent and the reassembled at the other end. Packets often include checksum codes to detect transmission errors. The exact layout of an individual packet is determined by the protocol being used.

■ packet switching

the method used to move data around on the Internet. In packet switching, all the data coming out of a machine is broken up into chunks, each chunk has the address of where it came from and where it is going. This enables chunks of data from many different sources to co-mingle on the same lines and be sorted and directed along different routes by special machines

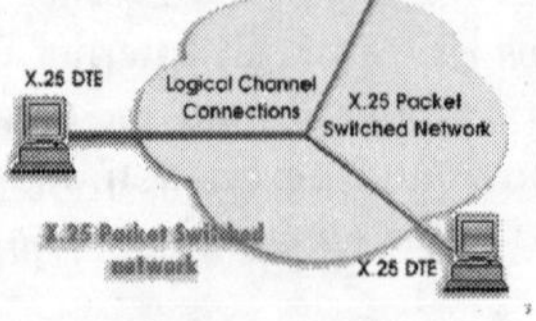

along the way. This way many people can use the same lines at the same time.
You might think of several caravans of trucks all using the same road system to carry materials.

page

1. to call somebody electronically. With telephone service, when you page someone, that person's pager activates and sounds an alarm. With the Internet, a page is usually a call to chat and will pop up a window on the recipient's desktop.
2. a document displayed on the web. A page may consist of a single screen or multiple screens reached by scrolling down or to the right.

page popularity

a measure of the number and quality of links to a particular page (inbound links). Many search engines are increasingly using this number as part of the positioning process. The number and quality of inbound links is becoming as important as the optimisation of page content.

page view

used in site statistics as a measure of pages viewed rather than server hits. Many server hits may be made to access a single page, causing many separate log file entries. Analysis software can determine that these server hits were generated when a visitor viewed a single page and group them together to provide this more useful method of counting visitors.

password, passcode

secret data item that is used to authenticate an entity. Passwords are often words that an individual is supposed to memorise, the system authenticates the person on the assumption that the password is only known by the person it belongs to.

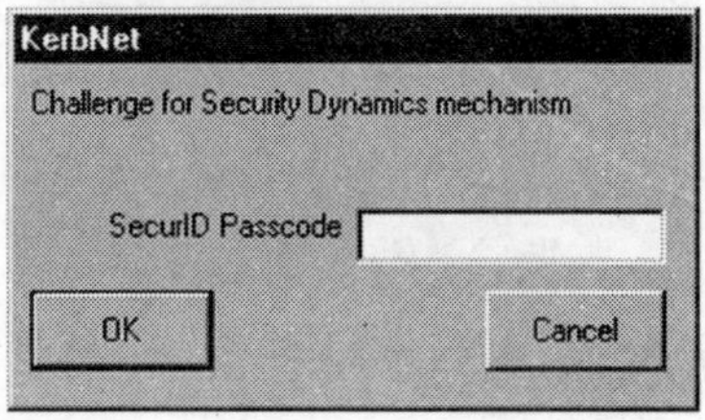

PC

a 'Personal Computer' that is compatible with the IBM desktop computers. PCs that are not manufactured by IBM Corporation are typically referred to as 'clones'. Generally, programs written on any PC will play on another PC. Most PC users now run under Microsoft DOS or Microsoft Windows operating systems. Newer and more advanced processors include OS/2 from IBM and Windows 2000 from Microsoft Corporation. Programs written on a Mac operating system will not usually run on a PC. Differences between Mac and PC computers have led to constant frustrations for authors since there is no single standard for authoring materials that can be used across the computer market. This is especially frustrating for authors of CD-ROM learning and entertainment materials. PC computers using the early Intel 8088 processor were called XT models.

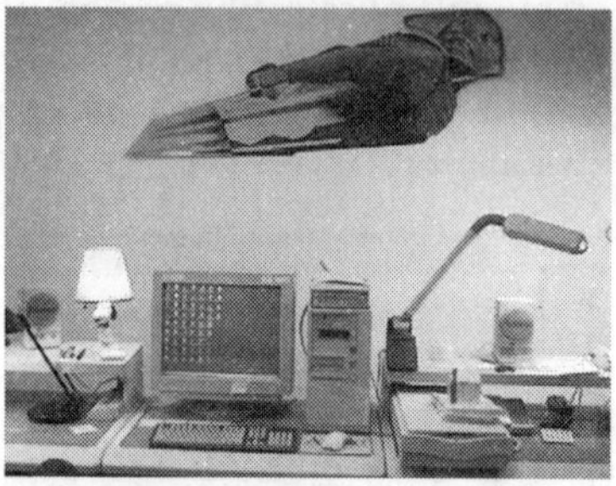

■ **PC card, pcmcia card**

a small, standard plug-in peripheral card often used in laptops as well as workstation computer systems. Modems are often packaged in PC cards. They are also used to hold crypto facilities and to safely store keying material.

■ **PDF**

Adobe's Portable Document Format. It is often used as a format, which allows much more complete, controlled layout of a page and its graphics and text than conventional HTML does. It requires a browser plug-in to see a web page in PDF format. Files will usually have a .pdf extension.

To create a page in PDF format, you need Adobe Acrobat (not the free Acrobat Reader) or other premium Adobe software. PhotoShop does. Adobe Illustrator does. PageMaker probably does.

■ **peeping tom**

attacker whose attacks are based on examining network data traffic: password sniffing, for example.

■ **personal page**

a web page created by an individual (as opposed to someone creating a page for an institution, business organisation or other entity). Often personal pages contain valid and useful opinions, links to important resources and significant facts. One of the greatest benefits of the Web is the freedom it as given almost anyone to put his or her ideas 'out there.' But frequently personal pages offer highly biased personal perspectives or ironical/satirical spoofs, which must be evaluated carefully. The presence in the page's URL of a personal name (such as 'jbarker') and a ~ or % or the word 'users' or 'people' or 'members' very frequently indicate a site offering personal pages.

■ **PHP**

a server-side, cross-platform, HTML embedded scripting language. This may sound a little foreign to all you folks coming from a non-Unix background, but PHP doesn't cost anything.

■ phrase

more than one Keyword, searched exactly as keyed (all terms required to be in documents, in the order keyed). Enclosing keywords in quotations ' ' forms a phrase in AltaVista and some other search tools. Some times a phrase is called a 'character string'.

■ PICS

Platform for Internet Content Selection. A model for associating labels with content in header metadata originally devised to help parents and teachers and filtering software control children's access to the net.

■ PING

Packet InterNet Groper. It is a program and UNIX command that helps testing and debugging network and/or Internet connections. An 'Echo' command is sent to a specified computer and then waits for a response. The result is a report that displays the success or failure, usually a report back of a timed response in seconds, of the intended action.

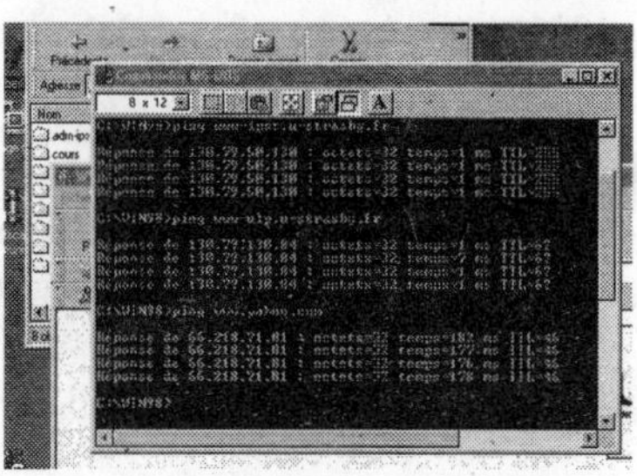

■ play-it-again sam

attacker whose attacks are based on intercepting legitimate messages and transmitting them over again in order to trick the system or its users somehow.

■ plug-in

a (usually small) piece of software that adds features to a larger piece of software. Common examples are plug-ins for the Netscape browser and web server.

■ PMFJIH

shorthand for 'Pardon Me For Jumping In Here'. Often used in chat and messages as a polite excuse to enter the discussion.

■ PNG

Portable Network Graphics. PNG is a graphics format specifically designed for use on the World Wide Web. PNG enable compression of images without any loss of quality, including high-resolution images. Another important feature of PNG is that anyone may create software that works with PNG images without paying any fees - the PNG standard is free of any licensing costs.

■ Point of Presence (POP)

a site that has a collection of telecommunications equipment, usually refers to ISP or telephone company sites.

■ Point-to-Point Protocol (PPP)

a protocol used by TCP/IP routers and PCs to send packets over dial-up and leased-line connections.

politeness window

in order not to overburden any particular server, most search engine spiders limit their access to each server. If your page is hosted on the same server as thousands of other pages, the spider may never get the time to reach (and index) your page. This can be a powerful argument for having your own server.

popularity ranking of search results

some search engines rank the order in which search results appear primarily by how many other sites link to each page (a kind of popularity vote based on the assumption that other pages would create a link to the 'best' pages). Google is the best example of this.

port

1. a place where information goes into or out of a computer or both. e.g. the serial port on a personal computer is where a *modem* would be connected.
2. on the Internet port often refers to a number that is part of a URL, appearing after a colon (:) right after the domain name. Every service on an Internet server listens on a particular port number on that server. Most services have standard port numbers, e.g. Web servers normally listen on port 80. Services can also listen on non-standard ports, in which case the port number must be specified in a URL when accessing the server, so you might see a URL of the form:
gopher:/ peg.cwis.uci.edu:7000/
This shows a gopher server running on a non-standard port (the standard gopher port is 70).
3. finally, port also refers to translating a piece of software to bring it from one type of computer system to another, e.g. to translate a Windows program so that is will run on a Macintosh.

port number

number carried in Internet transport protocols to identify which service or program is supposed to receive an incoming packet. Certain port numbers are permanently assigned to particular protocols by the IANA. For example, e-mail generally uses port 25 and Web services traditionally use port 80.

portal

usually used as a marketing term to describe a Web site that is or is intended to be the first place people see when using the Web. Typically a 'Portal site' has a catalogue of web sites, a search engine or both. A Portal site may also offer e-mail and other service to entice people to use that site as their main 'point of entry' (hence 'portal') to the Web.

positioning

the process of ordering web sites or web pages by a search engine or a directory so that the most relevant sites appear first in the search results for a particular query. Software such as PositionAgent, Rank This and Webposition can be used to determine how a URL is positioned for a particular search engine when using a particular search phrase. The GoHip Search site allows you to see positioning information from many of the big search engines, displayed all on one page.

■ positioning technique

a method of modifying a web page so that search engines (or a particular search engine) treat the page as more relevant to a particular query (or a set of queries).

■ post

to send a message to a public area like a BBS or newsgroup where it can be read by many others.

■ postmaster

the name given to the person in charge of administrating e-mail for a particular site.

■ power newbie

an enthusiastic newbie (network newcomer) who takes advantage of educational resources in an effort to become a knowbie. Power newbies share their knowledge with other newbies both face-to-face and in bulletin boards and chat rooms.

■ PPTP

Point to Point Tunnelling Protocol. A new technology developed by Microsoft, US Robotics and others to enable Virtual Private Networks (VPN) to work securely over the Internet without exposing their communications to intercept. It is currently available only to Windows NT and linux networks. As of June 2, 1998, security flaws have been revealed in Windows NT, which make it much less secure than previously believed. Security patches are expected.

■ Pretty Good Privacy (PGP)

a program, developed by Phil Zimmerman, that uses cryptography to protect files and electronic mail from being read by others. PGP also includes a feature, which allows users to digitally 'sign' a document or message, in order to provide non-forgable proof of authorship.

■ print queues

definitions of the order in which and where a file is to be printed on the network.

■ privacy

a source of concern to many on the Internet is how much personal information on them is available to all who look for it. Wherever you open an account on the Internet and World Wide Web, you are asked for personal information. What happens to this information? Do you have a right to privacy?

■ Privacy Enhanced Mail (PEM)

e-mail crypto protocol published by the IETF and provided in some commercial products. It has essentially been superceded by PGP, MSP and S/MIME.

■ **prodigy**

a commercial online service.

■ **program**

a series of instructions that tell a computer what to do. Also to create or revise a program.

■ **programmed attack**

attack on a computer device or protocol that can be embodied in a computer program. Such attacks can be used by attackers with limited expertise.

■ **protocol**

on the Internet 'protocol' usually refers to a set of rules that define an exact format for communication between systems. For example the HTTP protocol defines the format for communication between web browsers and web servers, the IMAP protocol defines the format for communication between IMAP e-mail servers and clients and the SSL protocol defines a format for encrypted communications over the Internet.

Virtually all Internet protocols are defined in RFC documents.

■ **protocol suite**

a collection of communications protocols that work together to provide useful services. There are two widely known protocol suites: the Internet protocols and the ISO/OSI protocols.

■ **proxy**

facility that indirectly provides some service. Proxy crypto applies crypto services to network traffic without individual hosts having to support the services themselves. Firewall proxies provide access to Internet services that are on the other side of the firewall while controlling access to services in either direction.

■ **proxy server**

a Proxy Server sits in between a Client and the 'real' Server that a Client is trying to use. Clients are sometimes configured to use a Proxy Server, usually an HTTP server. The clients makes all of it's requests from the Proxy Server, which then makes requests from the 'real' server and passes the result back to the Client. Sometimes the Proxy server will store the results and give a stored result instead of making a new one (to reduce use of a Network). Proxy servers are commonly established on Local Area Networks.

■ **push**

the technology that puts pre-selected content directly on your computer screen from the Internet without your need to browse for it. With this technology, introduced by PointCast and Individual, Inc. and added to 4th generation browsers, you can program your desktop, for example, to automatically receive such things as local weather, news headlines, selected stock reports and sports scores for selected teams or events.

■ query

1. a general question posed to a person or group over the Internet. Internet users are generally so helpful that if one asks an appropriate query to the correct discussion group, one will often receive many useful responses. One caveat: it is necessary to find and read the appropriate FAQ document first. Failure to do so would be considered a waste other people's time and bandwidth.

2. a request for specific information from a database.

■ queue

a sequence of items such as packets or print jobs waiting to be processed. For example, a print queue holds files that are waiting to be printed.

■ radio

Internet and satellite radio delivered by non-traditional media.

■ RADSL

acronym for Rate Adaptive Digital Subscriber Line, currently being introduced by US West. See **DSL**.

■ RAID

Redundant Arrays of Independent Disks. Using duplicated disks for error recovery and more efficient operation.

■ raw

Rutgers Accounting Web informational retrieval system (funded with a grant from NCAIR) for a variety of free materials for accounting educators. The main purpose of the system is to share materials developed in connection with the Accounting Education Change Commission (AECC). Materials include lectures, cases, assignments, examinations, syllabi and course outlines and reports of projects at various AECC sponsored sites. The World Wide Web address for the Lynx program for text only is <http//www.rutgers.edu/Accounting/raw.htm>. Lynx only transfers text. For graphics, a Mosaic option is available.

■ RDF

Resource Definition Framework. A set of rules (a sort of language) for creating descriptions of information, especially information available on the *World Wide Web*. RDF could be used to describe a collection of books or artists or a collection of *web pages* as in the *RSS* data format which uses RDF to create machine-readable summaries of web sites.

RDF is also used in *XPFE* applications to define the relationships between different collections of elements, for example RDF could be used to define the relationship between the data in a database and the way that data is displayed to a user.

■ RE, RE's

chat shorthand for 'rehi', meaning 'hello again'.

read receipts

an optional e-mail feature that notifies you when a recipient has opened the e-mail message you sent him.

readme file

1. a text file included with an application that contains important (and often last minute) information about installing and using the application.
2. a text file on an FTP site that provides valuable information about the context of site.
3. any text file that you are supposed to read before proceeding.

realnames

an alternate website address system in operation at Altavista. Brand names used in searches are mapped directly to the appropriate website, usually because the company owning the brand-name has paid a fee to RealNames. http://www.realnames.com

referrer

the URL of the web page from which a visitor came. The server's referrer log file will indicate this. If a visitor came directly from a search engine listing, the query used to find the page will usually be encoded in the referer URL, making it easy to see which keywords are bringing visitors. The referer information can also be accessed as document.referrer within JavaScript or via the HTTP_REFERER environment variable (accessible from scripting languages).

refresh

a meta tag that will let you either periodically refresh the current page or switch to another page. It is formatted like this:
<meta http-equiv='Refresh' content='10,
URL=http: www.waltho-we.com/
'>
The above meta tag will switch to the URL after 10 seconds. Change the number to change the time delay or delete it to make the change immediate. Delete the URL to make the refresh occur in the current page.

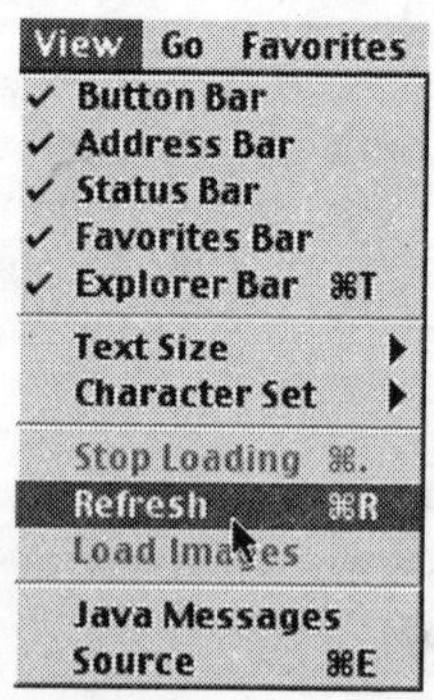

registration

the process of informing a search engine or directory that a new web page or web site should be indexed.

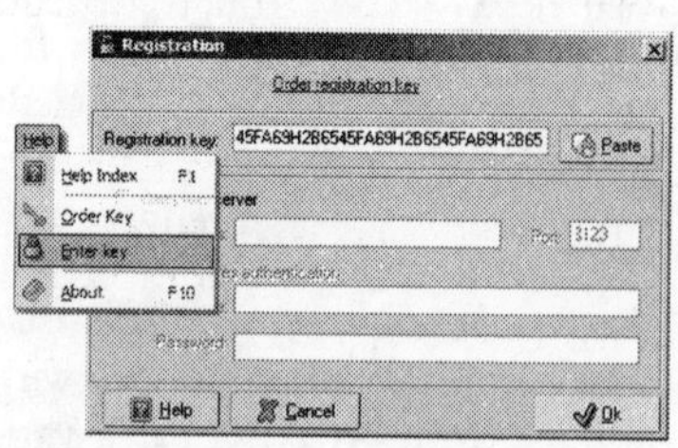

■ relevancy algorithm

the method a search engine or directory uses to match the keywords in a query with the content of each web page, so that the web pages found can be ordered suitably in the query results. Each search engine or directory is likely to use a different algorithm and to change or improve its algorithm from time to time.

■ remote login

operating a remote computer over a network as if it were a local computer. This can be accomplished via one of several protocols, including telnet and the UNIX program rlogin.

■ replay

attack that attempts to trick the system by retransmitting a legitimate message. Some protocols include anti-replay mechanisms to detect and reject such attacks.

■ response time

a measurement of the time between a request for information over a network and the network's fulfilment of that request. 'Overall response time' is an aggregate or average measurement of various response times over a particular network or through a particular host.

■ re-submission

repeating the search engine registration process one or more times for the same page or site. Under certain circumstances, this is regarded with suspicion by the search engines, as it could indicate that someone is experimenting with spamming techniques.

The Infoseek and Altavista search engines are particularly vulnerable to spamming because they list sites very quickly and are thus easy to experiment with. Both engines delist sites for repeated re-submission and Infoseek, for example, does not allow more than one submission of the same page in a 24 hour period. Occasional re-submission of changed pages is not normally a problem.

■ reusable password

password that can be used over and over, as opposed to a one time password. Most passwords used today are reusable passwords.

■ Reverse Address Resolution Protocol (RARP)

Reverse Address Resolution Protocol is a protocol by which a physical machine in a local area network can request to learn its IP address from a gateway server's Address Resolution Protocol (Address Resolution Protocol) table or cache. A network administrator creates a table in a local area network's gateway router that maps the physical machine (or Media Access Control - MAC address) addresses to corresponding Internet Protocol addresses. When a new machine is set up, its RARP client program requests from the RARP server on the router to be sent its IP address. Assuming that an entry has been set up in the router table, the RARP server will return the IP address to the machine which can store it for future use. RARP is available for Ethernet, Fibre Distributed-Data Interface and token ring LANs.

■ **reverse lookup**

a telephone directory service where, given the phone number, you can look up the name.

■ **rewrite**

attack that modifies an encrypted message's contents without decrypting it first.

■ **RFC (Request for Comments)**

the name of the result and the process for creating a standard on the Internet. New standards are proposed and published on the Internet, as a Request For Comments. The proposal is reviewed by the Internet Engineering Task Force (http://www.ietf.org/), a consensus-building body that facilitates discussion and eventually a new standard is established, but the reference number/name for the standard retains the acronym RFC, e.g. the official standard for *e-mail* message formats is RFC 822.

■ **RGB**

RGB is short for the colours red, green and blue often used in colour coding on web pages, particularly for GIF files. 64K colour values can be represented by a byte (8 bits of data) each for red, green and blue. These are commonly expressed in hexadecimal values from 00 too FF for each colour. The colour value for white in this system is FFFFFF, where each colour is at maximum value. Red is FF0000. Yellow is FFFF00. There is a smaller set of non-dithering colours where the permissible values for each colour are hexadecimal 00, 33, 66, 99, CC or FF or decimal 0, 51, 102, 153, 204 and 255 and the results will look the same with different browsers, computers and colour cards.

■ **Rich-Text Format (RTF)**

a text formatting standard established by Microsoft Corporation to enable text to be transferred between a word processor and other software without losing all of its formatting properties. Many modern word processors have the option of saving documents in rich-text format (RTF). Increasingly, authoring software vendors of hypertext, hypermedia and CMS software are adding RTF importing utilities to overcome the frustrations of importing in ASCII or ANSI forms that lose all or most formatting properties.

■ **ring topology**

a network configuration (topology) in which all computers and devices are connected to a circular pathway.

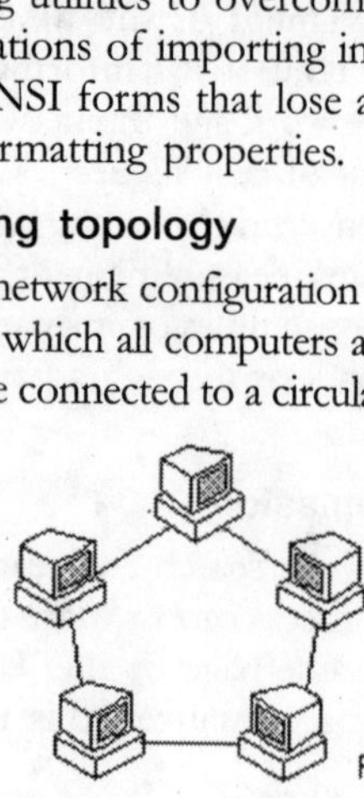

Ring

robot

any browser program which follows hypertext links and accesses web pages but is not directly under human control. Examples are the search engine spiders, the 'harvesting' programs which extract e-mail addresses and other data from web pages and various intelligent web searching programs. A database of web robots is maintained by Webcrawler.

robots.txt

a text file stored in the top level directory of a web site to deny access by robots to certain pages or sub-directories of the site. Only robots which comply with the *Robots Exclusion Standard* will read and obey the commands in this file. Robots will read this file on each visit, so that pages or areas of sites can be made public or private at any time by changing the content of robots.txt before re-submitting to the search engines.

ROTFL

abbreviation for 'Rolling On The Floor Laughing'.

router

a special-purpose computer (or software package) that handles the connection between 2 or more Packet-Switched networks. Routers spend all their time looking at the source and destination addresses of the packets passing through them and deciding which route to send them on.

routing host

a host that routes IP packets between networks as well as providing other services.

RPC

'Remote Procedure Call'. Protocol that allows a program on one computer to execute a program on a server computer. Using RPC, a system developer need not develop specific procedures for the server. With RPC you call a specific function whereas with an ORB you call a method within a distributed object. In ORB each object manages its own private instance of the data whereas in RPC you can only call a specific function and all functions get implemented in the same way. ORB allows for differential processing.

RSN

chat shorthand for 'real soon now'. It represents an indefinite period of time somewhat longer than the time 'the check is in the mail.'

RSS — (Rich Site Summary or RDF Site Summary or Real Simple Syndication)

a commonly used protocol for syndication and sharing of content. RSS is an XML-based summary of a web site, usually used for syndication and other kinds of content-sharing. There are RSS 'feeds' which are sources of RSS information about web sites and RSS 'readers' which read RSS feeds and display their content to users.

RTFM

chat shorthand for 'read the fine manual'.

S/MIME

Secure Multipart Internet Message Extensions. Proposed protocol for embedding crypto protected messages in Internet e-mail.

SAN

Storage Area Network. A high speed network of shared storage devices.

scalability

how well a system performs as it grows. For example, a central server of some kind with ten clients may perform efficiently. It has a scalability problem if it fails with an increasing number of clients. If the average response time probably scales linearly with the number of clients, it has a complexity of O(N) ('order N'). It has been described as 'Web-enabled database which potentially lets customers scale from desktop or laptop systems to massively parallel processors'.

scanner

both hand-held and flatbed hardware and software for copying graphics images and text into computer files. Both colour and black and white options are available. People seldom have had much luck with hand-held versions, but flatbed scanners do a terrific job. Text scanned as graphics must be converted into computer text via specialised software such as Omni Page Pro from Caere (800-GO-CAERE). see also **OCR**.

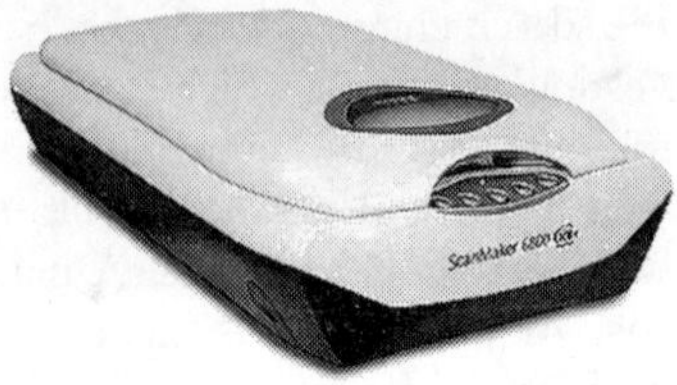

script

a script is a type of programming language that can be used to fetch and display Web pages. There are may kinds and uses of scripts on the Web. They can be used to create all or part of a page and communicate with searchable databases. Forms (boxes) and many interactive links, which respond differently depending on what you enter, all require some kind of script language. When you find a question mark (?) in the URL of a page, some kind of script command was used in generating and/or delivering that page. Most search engine spiders are instructed not to crawl pages from scripts, although it is usually technically possible for them to do so.

scroll (down, up, left, right)

moving up or down within a document in your screen. Use scroll bar at right. Click on arrow down or arrow up. Drag the scroll button down or up. Or click on the page up or page down icons at the bottom of the bar. If you need to scroll left or right, use the scroll bar at the bottom.

■ scrolling

scrolling the chat screen is when you type in a single letter or symbol in the compose area and keep hitting send. This scrolls the chat screen very quickly and disrupts the chat conversation for others. This is very bad Netiquette and against the rules established for most chat rooms.

■ SDSL

Symmetric Digital Subscriber Line. A version of DSL where the upload speeds and download speeds are the same.

■ search engine

a utility that will search the Internet, an Intranet, a site or a database for terms that you select. Search engines on the web consist of four elements:

a program that roams the area to be searched, collecting data records (typically, web pages) and links to more data. These are variously known as spiders, worms, crawlers or other colourful names. Commercial databases, on the other hand, may collect data records in other ways, such as systematically entering the full text of newspapers or journals. A database or collection of records recovered by the spiders or other type of collector. An index of the database collected to enable fast access to terms that you search for and their supporting records. Indexes may be enhanced by controlled vocabularies. A search interface- the form in which you enter your search terms and the software behind it that queries the index, retrieves matches and ranks for relevance and organises the data for follow-on searches.

Each of the major search engines differs in its approach to these four elements.

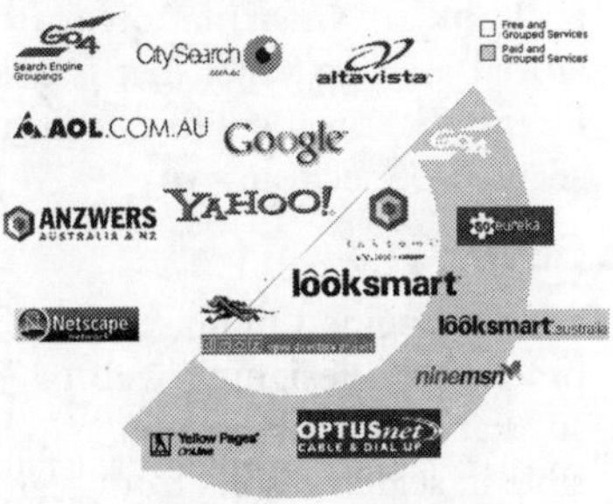

■ searchking

a smaller search engine which allows visitors to vote on the relevance of the pages returned by their queries, thus ranking sites based on the opinions of searchers. Unlike some of the major search engines, there is good customer support. http://www.searchking.com.

■ secret key

crypto key that is used in a secret key ('symmetric') algorithm. The secrecy of encrypted data depends solely on the secrecy of the secret key.

■ secret key algorithm

crypto algorithm that uses the same key to encrypt data and to decrypt data. Also called a 'symmetric' algorithm.

security

ensuring that private information remains private in an atmosphere where all other information is free. Security also means that viruses are prevented from infecting people's systems.

security certificate

a chunk of information (often stored as a text file) that is used by the SSL protocol to establish a secure connection.

SEO

Search Engine Optimisation. The practice of designing web pages so that they rank as high as possible in search results from search engines.

There is 'good' SEO and 'bad' SEO. Good SEO involves making the web page clearly describe its subject, making sure it contains truly useful information, including accurate information in *Meta tags* and arranging for other web sites to make links to the page. Bad SEO involves attempting to deceive people into believing the page is more relevant than it truly is by doing things like adding inaccurate Meta tags to the page.

server

a computer or a software package, that provides a specific kind of service to client software running on other computers. The term can refer to a particular piece of software, such as a WWW server or to the machine on which the software is running, e.g. 'Our mail server is down today, that's why e-mail isn't getting out'.

A single server machine can (and often does) have several different server software packages running on it, thus providing many different servers to clients on the network.

Sometimes server software is designed so that additional capabilities can be added to the main program by adding small programs known as servlets.

server-side

something that operates on the 'server' computer (providing the Web page), as opposed to the 'client' computer (which is you or someone else viewing the Web page). Usually it is a program or command or procedure or other application causes dynamic pages or animation or other interaction.

service provider

a company that provides dial-up or direct access to the Internet for a fee. Sometimes referred to as ISP (Internet Service Provider).

servlet

a small computer program designed to be add capabilities to a larger piece of server software. Common examples are 'Java servlets', which are small programs written in the Java language and which are added to a *web* server. Typically a web server that uses Java servlets will have many of them, each one designed to handle a very specific situation, for example one servlet will handle adding items to a 'shopping cart', while a different servlet will handle deleting items from the 'shopping cart'.

■ session key

crypto key intended to encrypt data for a limited period of time, typically only for a single communications session between a pair of entities. Once the session is over, the key will be discarded and a new one established when a new session takes place. Also called a data key.

■ set-top box

a digital device that will sit on top of or inside a television set and provide the digital processing necessary to support interactive network services (video-on-demand, network placing of purchase orders, database access, etc.) in the early phases of the information highway. Eventually PCTVs will probably replace set-top box processors.

■ SGML

acronym for Standard Generalised Markup Language. It was adopted in 1986 as an international standard (ISO 8879) for the creation, management, storage and delivery of information products. HTML and its possible successor, XML, are both subsets of SGML.

■ shareware

software that you can download from a network and 'try before you buy'. If you like the software and decide to use it beyond the trial period, you must register with the author and pay a registration fee. If you don't wish to register as a user, you are often required to remove the software from your computer.

■ shell

web server/client software focused on storage, delivery and course management. This software facilitates server/client networking that allows for student record keeping, test grading, etc. Unlike high-end authoring software, courseware shells have utilities for creating network listservs, bulletin boards, chat rooms, electronic forums, telephony, etc. These shells also facilitate lesson authoring in virtually all of the high-end authoring software listed above. Some courseware shells have more authoring capabilities than others, although none have the full authoring capabilities of the high-end authoring systems.

■ shim

a software component inserted at a well known interface between two other software components. 'Shim' versions of IPSEC are often implemented at the device driver interface, below the host's TCP/IP network protocol stack.

■ SHTTP

Secure Hypertext Transfer Protocol. Extension to HTTP to apply crypto services to Web data and transactions.

■ sig

1. abbreviation for Special Interest Group.

2. short for signature, a group of lines attached to the end of a message that identifies the author and often includes additional information such as contact information organisational affiliation or a favourite quote. Sigs can also include ASCII art. Netiquette suggests limiting sigs to a maximum of four or five lines.

■ silicon valley

the geographic centre of the computer industry. Includes most of Santa Clara county and part of San Mateo county in California.

■ similar to a chat environment

where the players assume the identities of fictional characters and follow a series of rules which guide the adventure.

■ Simple Key Interchange Protocol (SKIP)

protocol that establishes session keys to use with IPSEC protocol headers. SKIP data is carried in packet headers and travel in every IPSEC protected packet.

■ siphoning

the use of various means to steal another site's traffic. Techniques used include the wholesale copying of web pages (with the copied page altered slightly to direct visitors to a different site and then registered with the search engines) and the use of keywords or keyword phrases 'belonging' to other organisations, companies or web sites.

■ site

a host on the Internet which allows remote access by such protocols as http, ftp, telnet or gopher. A site may consist of a single page or many pages under a common site name. Whether two addresses with a common site name are one site or more than one may vary depending on your point of view. For example, to some, all pages at the Internet Service Provider delphiforums.com might be considered one site. But an individual who has set up personal web pages at people.delphiforums.com will refer to his or her pages as 'my web site'.

■ skewing

artificially changing search engine results so that, for example, popular queries will return artificially created listings. Infoseek is currently experimenting with this technique, using a small group of reviewers to artificially force higher relevance for certain sites.

■ skipjack

Block cipher developed by NSA and provided in the CAPSTONE, CLIPPER and FORTEZZA devices.

■ slam, slamming

slamming is the practice of telephone companies shifting you to their long distance service without your permission or obtaining your permission deceptively.

■ SLIP

Serial Line Internet Protocol. A protocol that allows users in selected parts of the world to access the Internet via modems and phone lines if they are not directly connected to the Internet system of worldwide networks. There are specialised SLIP firms plus some of the more general firms such as Delphi and CompuServe. Unlike direct connections, however, SLIP interfacings normally have usage fees based upon timing and extent of usage.

■ slurp

the name of the spider used by Inktomi.

■ smart agent

a utility for scanning Internet resources and collecting files pertinent to selected interests. This also includes screen savers that collect information (e.g., news is downloaded at assigned intervals on the Pointcast screen saver at <http://www.pointcast.com/>). See also **XML** and **search engine**.

■ SMDS

Switched Multimegabit Data Service. A new standard for very high-speed data transfer.

■ smiley

see **emoticon**.

■ smiley face

a happy face or other expression formed with typed characters, usually viewed by tilting your head to the left. These are used in place of real facial expressions, body language and tone of voice when writing. Also known as 'emoticon'.

:-) the basic smiley
;-) a wink
8-(unhappy
=|:-)= with glasses Uncle Sam

■ SMITS

Self-Monitoring Intelligent Tutoring System for computer-aided instruction of accounting information systems. SMITS was developed with an NCAIR grant.

■ SMTP

Simple Mail Transfer Protocol. The protocol used to send mail between servers and to send mail from your client to a mail server. Your address to send mail using software like Eudora, Pegasus or the mail clients in Netscape and MSIE will often begin with SMTP. For Delphi, the address to send mail through is smtp.delphiforums.com.

■ SNA

Systems Network Architecture

■ snail mail

regular postal mail, as opposed to e-mail. Pejorative when implying postal mail's slowness relative to e-mail.

snake oil

derogatory term applied to a product whose developers describe it with misleading, inconsistent or incorrect technical statements.

snap!

a large directory. The URL is http://www.snap.com.

sneakernet

the transfer of electronic information by physically carrying disks, tape or some other media from one machine to another. Used ironically.

sniffer

the name of the filter program used by the Infoseek search engine to prevent spamdexing. It detects multiple mirror pages, font and background spoofs, multiple title tags, keyword stuffing and possibly other types of spamdexing.

sniffing

attack that collects information from network messages by making copies of their contents. Password sniffing is the most widely publicised example.

SNMP

Simple Network Management Protocol. A standard for management of devices such as hubs, routers and switches attached to an IP network. It operates at the application layer of the OSI Model.

SOAP

Simple Object Access Protocol. A protocol for client-server communication that sends and receives information on top of' HTTP. The data sent and received is in a particular XML format specifically designed for use with SOAP. SOAP is similar to the XMLRPC protocol except that SOAP provides for more sophisticated handling of complex data being sent between a client and a server. SOAP actually grew from the work that created XMLRPC.

Microsoft's '.NET' system is largely based on SOAP.

social engineering

a cracker term for tricking users of a system to reveal passwords so that the cracker can gain entry to the system. A common technique is to contact users in chat or e-mail on a system, pretend that they are employees of the system performing security checks and insist that the users give their password to prove who they are or their account will be closed. Such requests are never legitimate! Social engineering schemes can be quite ingenious and convincing and more subtle than the simple technique above. Never reveal a password or even give hints what it may be.

socket

this is a communication mechanism originally implemented on the BSD version of the UNIX operating system. Sockets are used as endpoints for sending and receiving data between computers. A SSL (secure socket layer) is a secured security socket that controls data flows into and out of a socket for security purposes.

■ socket interface

the software interface between a host's network protocol stack and applications programs that use the network.

■ SOHO

acronym for Small Office, Home Office.

■ solaris

see **Unix**.

■ SONET

Synchronised Optical Network that is now operational on 155 Mb per second fibre optic cable between major cities in the United States. This forms the AT&T Corporation backbone for asynchronous transfer mode (ATM) switching and transmission of voice, video, graphics and data. see also **information highway, fibre optic** and **networks.**

■ sound board

a hardware insert for computers that allows mono or stereo audio (e.g., from cassette players, microphones and television audio tracks) to be sent to computer speakers 'on the fly' and/or to be captured as computer files such aswav and voc files for PC computers. The wav file extensions run on Microsoft MCI standards and the voc files run on Soundblaster sound boards from Creative Labs.

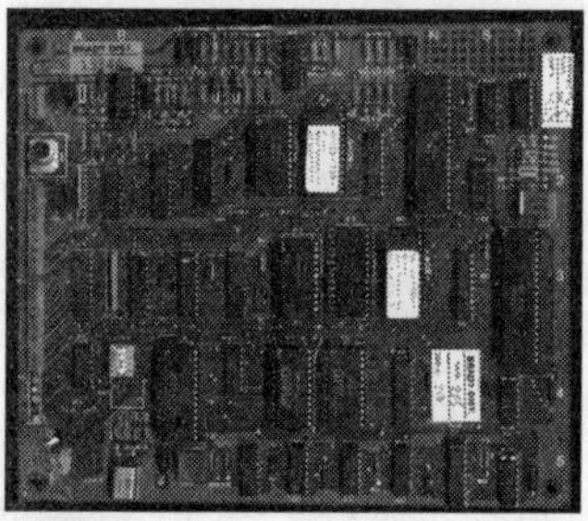

■ spam

to send a message (usually an advertisement) to many discussion groups (bulletin boards, mailing lists and/or newsgroups), without regard for its topical relevance. The act of spamming was pioneered in 1994 by Canter & Siegel, the immigration lawyers who sent an advertisement for their services to every USENET newsgroup and received a whole lot of flamage in return.

■ spamdexing

the alteration or creation of a document with intent to deceive an electronic catalogue or filing system. Any technique that increases the potential position of a site at the expense of the quality of the search engine's database can also be regarded as spamdexing

- also known as spamming or spoofing.

■ sparc

a class of Unix-based workstations from Sun Microsystems. These are common in Unix-based networks. see also **SUN**.

■ speech recognition

the ability of the computer to interpret speech or other audio commands along with keyboard, mouse and joystick commands.

■ spidering

the process of surfing the web, storing URLs and indexing keywords, links and text. Typically, even the largest search engines cannot spider all of the pages on the net. This is due to the huge amount of data available, the speed at which the new data appears, the use of politeness windows and practical limits on the number of pages that can be visited in a given time . The search engines have to make compromises in order to visit as many sites as possible and they do this in different ways. For example, some only index the home pages of each site, some only visit sites they're explicitly told about and some make judgements about the importance of sites (from number and quality of inbound links) before 'digging deeper' into the subpages of a site.

■ spiders

computer robot programs, referred to sometimes as 'crawlers' or 'knowledge-bots' or 'knowbots' that are used by search engines to roam the World Wide Web via the Internet, visit sites and databases and keep the search engine database of web pages up to date. They obtain new pages, update known pages and delete obsolete ones. Their findings are then integrated into the 'home' database. Most large search engines operate several robots all the time. Even so, the Web is so enormous that it can take six months for spiders to cover it, resulting in a certain degree of 'out-of-datedness' (link rot) in all the search engines. For more information, read about search engines.

■ splash page

similar to a gateway page but provides an initial display which must be viewed before a visitor reaches the main page. This usually acts as a kind of 'opening title' sequence and can be extremely annoying.

■ splitting

dividing a crypto key into two separate keys so that an attacker can not reconstruct the actual crypto key even if one of the split keys is intercepted.

■ sponsor (of a web page or site)

many Web pages have organisations, businesses, institutions like universities or non-profit foundations or other interests which 'sponsor' the page. Frequently you can find a link titled

'Sponsors' or an 'About us' link explaining who or what (if anyone) is sponsoring the page. Sometimes the advertisers on the page (banner ads, links, buttons to sites that sell or promote something) are 'sponsors.' WHY is this important? Sponsors and the funding they provide may or may not, influence what can be said on the page or site - can bias what you find, by excluding some opposing viewpoint or causing some other imbalanced information. The site is not bad because of sponsors, but you they should alert you to the need to evaluate a page or site very carefully.

■ spoofing

see **spamdexing**.

■ spool

a queue of files waiting to be printed.

■ sprayer

a computer program designed to serve web pages from multiple hosts in order to optimise traffic between the hosts.

■ spread spectrum transmission

a technique that takes a narrow signal and spreads it over a broader portion of the radio frequency band. Unlicensed National Information Infrastructure (U-NII) Band: An unregulated radio frequency that uses the 5 GHz band for communication, this band is divided into three sub-bands and are intended for use by short-range, high-speed wireless digital communication devices.

■ sprite

an independent graphic object that moves freely across the screen.

■ spyware

software planted on your system to capture and reveal information to someone outside your system. It can do such things as capture your keystrokes while typing passwords, read and track your e-mail, record what sites you visit, pass along credit card numbers and so on. It can be planted by Trojan horses or viruses, installed as part of freeware or shareware programs you download and run, installed by an employer to track your computer usage or even planted by advertising agencies to assist in feeding you targeted ads.

■ SQL

Structured Query Language. A specialised language for sending queries to databases. Most industrial-strength and many smaller database applications can be addressed using SQL. Each specific application will have its own slightly different version of SQL implementing features unique to that application, but all SQL-capable databases support a common subset of SQL. A example of an SQL statement is:
SELECT name,e-mail FROM people_table WHERE country= 'uk'

■ SSA

Serial Storage Architecture, along with its FC-AL Fibre Channel alternative, that offer huge bandwidth networking schemes that operate within an Eithernet network. Shared discs in SSA or FC-AL systems can be operated over networks as fast as hard drives on a local computer. Furthermore, the connecting cables are 'thin' relative to traditional SCSI connection cables. While Ultra-Wide SCSI has a 40Mbps maximum bandwidth, SSA offers 80 MBps and FC-AL goes up to 100 MBps. SSA is fully duplex with two cables to devices. One advantage of SSA is that if a connected device fails, the entire loop does not fail since SSA does not require a hub. Over time, SSA systems and FC-AL will probably replace SCSI systems.

■ SSI commands

SSI stands for 'server-side include', a type of HTML instruction telling a computer that serves Web pages to dynamically generate data, usually by inserting certain variable contents into a fixed template or boilerplate Web page. Used especially in database searches.

■ SSL

Secure Sockets Layer. A security protocol developed by Netscape for commercial transactions on the Internet. Using public-key cryptography, it provides server authentication, data encryption and data integrity. You can recognise its use with URLs beginning https instead of http.

■ stage directions

used in chats to indicate vocal inflections, facial expressions or body language. Usually surrounded by < > , for example < grin > and < hug >.

■ star/ star topology

a network configuration (topology) in which all computers and

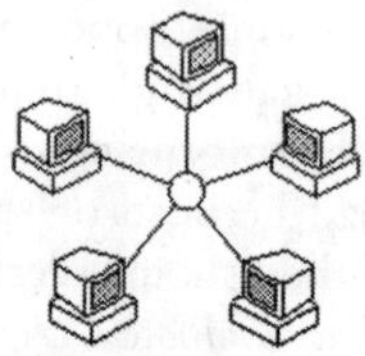

Star

devices are connected by direct cables to a central hub.

■ status bar

a bar at the bottom of a window that is used to indicate the status of a task. For example, when you send an e-mail message, you'll see the status bar filling with dots indicating that your message is being sent.

■ stealth script

a CGI script which switches page content depending on who or what is accessing the page.

■ stemming

in keyword searching, word endings are automatically removed (*lines* becomes *line*), searches are performed on the stem + common endings (line or lines retrieves line, lines, line's, lines', lining, lined). Not very common as a practice and not always disclosed. Can usually be avoided by placing a term in ' '.

■ stop

button at end of Netscape's Tool Button Bar. Use to stop downloading of a document.

■ stop word

a word which is ignored in a query because the word is so commonly used that it makes no contribution to relevancy. Examples are common net words such as computer and web and general words like get, I, me, the and you.

■ streaming audio, streaming video

technologies which permit listening and watching continuously as the signal is transferred to your system from a remote web site. It requires a high degree of compression to transfer audio or video (or both) at 28.8 Kbps or 14.4 Kbps speeds and still retain quality music and non-jerky video. If stereo sound is desired, there is a trade-off in the sound quality. These technologies are continually improving and the sound and video sampling and compression techniques are getting better. Faster connection speeds are needed to improve quality substantially and the speed must be maintained over the entire path between the transmitting and receiving systems. The systems generally use a few seconds buffering, but signal slowdowns or interruptions longer than that break the flow.

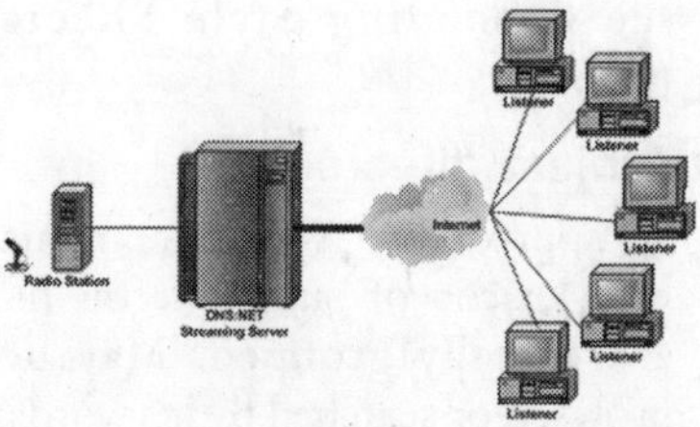

■ strong crypto

crypto facilities that exceed the standards for lightweight or medium strength crypto and therefore face significant restrictions under U. S. export rules.

■ structured

this adjective describes how data are stored and used at companies. Travel agents, for example, type information into designated spaces on electronic forms on their computer screens that are connected to database programs. That structures or categorises, the information so it can be searched and sorted using such criteria as a customer's name or destination. The Web, in contrast, stores data in an unstructured way that limits the kinds of searches that can be performed.

■ student response pads

hand-held wireless audience response pads which allow individual answers or group frequency responses to be immediately displayed in front of the class. The pads themselves must be separately purchased. HyperGraphics is the only CMS vendor that sells response pads with built in CMS software utilities.

style sheet

see **Cascading Style Sheets (CSS)**.

subject directory

an approach to Web documents by a lexicon of subject terms hierarchically grouped. May be browsed or searched by keywords. Subject directories are smaller than other searchable databases, because of the human involvement required to classify documents by subject.

submission service

any agent which submits your site to many search engines and directories. Useful to get listed with many of the minor search engines, but don't rely on such services to get listed with the major search engines. Many of these services are automatic and run from web sites. Others run offline. Some are free. Beware of supplying your e-mail address to the so-called FFA (free for all) services - you may receive lots of spam.

subroutine

a piece of a program that is 'called' from another part of the program. Often a well-structured program will consist of a short main routine that calls many subroutines to do the work.

subscribe

to add one's name to a mailing list.

sub-searching

ability to search only within the results of a previous search. Enables you to refine search results, in effect making the computer 'read' the search results for you selecting documents with terms you sub-search on. Can function much like Results Ranking.

Sun

Sun Microsystem computers, most of which are network workstations using Unix operating systems. The Sun Microsystems SPARClassic M (under $5,000) and 10SX (over $15,000) are designed to compete with the SGI Indago line for multimedia computing.

surf

to explore the nets without any more specific a purpose than to see what is out there.

surge protector

a device, usually in the form of a multi-plug bar, that protects your computer from being damaged by power surges.

SVG

open-standard vector graphics format that lets you add high-quality graphics and animation to Web pages using plain text commands. It's the powerful combination of dynamic two-dimensional vector graphics and Extensible Markup Language (XML). Simply put, SVG creates small file sizes for faster Web page downloads, offers unlimited colour and font choices and that's just the beginning.

switched network

is the opposite of dedicated bandwidth on the information highway. It is analogous to having a bridge that opens certain lanes in one direction to accommodate traffic flows in the morning rush hours and then changes the directions to accommodate evening rush traffic. In the case of switched networks, the bandwidth dedicated to flows of data, voice, video and audio can be changed as needed. For example, video may require a temporary widening that limits data and audio flows. see also **bandwidth, information highway** and **video server**.

symmetric algorithm

crypto algorithm that uses the same crypto key for encrypting and decrypting. Also called a 'secret key' algorithm.

synchronous connection

an analog to analog or digital to digital connection that is able to perform two or more processes at the same time by means of a mutual timing signal or clock.

syntax

the rules of construction and terminology of a computer programming language. These rules are analogous to rules of spelling and grammar in a language, except that syntax rules are usually less forgiving. We can read a thousand-page book that has one error in spelling or grammar. Such is not the case with a computer program because it will not usually run if there is a syntax error.

sysadmin

the system administrator of a UNIX machine or someone who maintains UNIX systems.

sysop

a system operator, usually the administrative manager of a BBS, mailing list or newsgroup, who manages the day-to-day administrative tasks and makes sure the technical features work.

Systems Network Architecture (SNA)

a proprietary networking architecture used by IBM and IBM-compatible mainframe computers.

T-1

a leased-line connection capable of carrying data at 1,544,000 *bits*-per-second. At maximum theoretical capacity, a T-1 line could move a megabyte in less than 10 seconds. That is still not fast enough for full-screen, full-motion video, for which you need at least 10,000,000 bits-per-second. T-1 lines are commonly used to connect large LANs to the Internet.

T3

a high speed, high bandwidth leased line connection to the Internet. T3 connections deliver information at 44.746 megabits per second.

tag

in reference to web pages, a tag is an HTML command used in laying out a web page and providing links to resources.

■ Taligent

a former software development venture initially commenced by Apple and IBM corporations. In 1994, Hewlett-Packard announced it would take 15% in Taligent and provide technical support. Taligent's primary mission is to develop cross-platform object-oriented operating systems and applications software, the first release of which will be in 1995 for IBM's Unix-based system called AIX. Versions for OS/2, PowerOpen and Hewlett-Packards HP-UX systems will follow. The future of Taligent along with a similar joint venture at Kaleida Labs is somewhat uncertain due to changing times and top management strategies in IBM and Apple according to a famous magazine. Key features of the Taligent applications operating system and the 'People, Places and Things' user interface are discussed in Panettieri (1994b). The key feature is the object-oriented design that will greatly reduce the time and effort needed by software developers who can make use of chunks of pre-written code.

In 1996, Taligent seemed beaten up and dead in the water until IBM decided to put an enormous investment into Java support. In 1997, Taligent became the industry leader in Java development.

■ TCP

stands for Transmission Control Protocol. Both the protocol and software that ensure that data sent over the Net arrive in the correct order.

■ TCP/IP

Transmission Control Protocol/ Internet Protocol. The protocols that are the basis for transmitting and routing data packets on the Internet. The Internet Protocol is the one thing that all current Internet sites have in common. The basic TCP/IP model has five layers of interaction:

Physical or Data Transport Layer. This most basic layer moves data over cables based on the physical address of each Network Interface Card (NIC). The most common types are ethernet and token ring.

Data Link Layer. This layer frames the packets of data that are sent through the network. PPP, frame relay and X.25 operate at this layer. Bridges connect local networks at this layer.

Network or Internet Protocol Layer. This layer puts an Internet Protocol wrapper around the data with source and destination addresses in its header. Routers, which connect networks together, operate at this layer.

Transport Layer. This layer governs the setting of suitable packet sizes, segmenting and reassembling data, detection of errors and flow control.

Application Layer. This layer provides for standard interfaces for such functions as message handling and file transfer and remote login. It allows, for example, for different e-mail programs to be used, as long as they conform to the standard interface. This layer in TCP/IP corresponds to the session, presentation and application layers in the OSI model.

■ TDMA

Time Division Multiple Access. TDMA is a method of dividing a single analog channel into a number of time slots and assigning each user a distinct time slot within a given channel. This lets more users (usually three) access a channel at one time without interference. TDMA is one of the standard digital cellular technologies, along with CDMA. GSM is a variant.

■ telecommunications

the science of sending signals representing voice, video or data through telephone lines.

■ telecommuting

to work at home and use a computer and modem to communicate with the office.

■ teleconference

a telephone communication in which more than two people are simultaneously connected so they can exchange verbal comments as if they were in the same room having a face-to-face conference. A teleconference need not have visual communications in addition to audio communications, but modern technology now makes it possible to see conference members on monitor screens or television screens. see also **IRC** and **videoconferencing**.

■ teledildonics

sex in a computer simulated environment. While it's not yet possible, except in conversational form in chat rooms and MUDs, it remains a future possibility.

■ telematics

the combination of computers in concert with telecommunications systems. This includes dial-up service to the Internet as well as all types of networks that rely on a telecommunications system to transport data.

■ telephony

real time telephone conversation across a network, especially networks on the Internet. see **chat lines** and **IRC.**

■ television

see **video.**

■ telnet

the Internet standard protocol for remote login service that allows users on the Internet to access programs and applications on computers in remote locations. Telnet allows a user at one site to interact with a remote timesharing system at another site as if the user's terminal were connected directly to the remote computer. When using the Internet, type 'Telnet' followed by a space and the address of the computer for remote login. Note that the Telnet protocol should not be confused with the Telnet public data network. see also **protocol** and **remote login.**

■ **teotwawki**

acronym of 'The End of The World As We Know It'. Perhaps invented by those pessimistic about the Year 2000.

■ **terabyte**

1000 gigabytes.

■ **terminal**

a device that allows you to send commands to a computer somewhere else. At a minimum, this usually means a keyboard and a display screen and some simple circuitry. Usually you will use terminal software in a personal computer - the software pretends to be (emulates) a physical terminal and allows you to type commands to a computer somewhere else.

■ **terminal server**

a special purpose computer that has places to plug in many modems on one side and a connection to a LAN or *host* machine on the other side. Thus the terminal server does the work of answering the calls and passes the connections on to the appropriate *node*. Mostterminal servers can provide PPP or SLIP services if connected to the Internet.

■ **text box**

a box into which you can type text.

■ **text reading**

the conversion of computer text into audio sounds. The flip side of 'speech recognition' is 'text reading' conversion of written text into audio. The pioneer in this technology is Bell Labs at http://www.islip.com/. That Bell Labs web site has some wonderful demonstrations of this technology. Apple Computer has a text manager in its AV models. Options such as Text Assist from Creative Labs (800-998-1000) and related hardware/software from sound board vendors are available for PCs.

■ **text recognition**

see **text reading.**

■ **texture**

texturing effects in graphics images and multimedia backgrounds. Comparisons of software options for 'tantalising textures' are compared in a famous magazine.

■ **thesaurus**

in some search tools, the terms you choose to search on can lead you to other terms you may not have thought of. Different search tools have different ways of presenting this information, sometimes with suggested words you may choose among and sometimes automatically. The terms are based on the terms in the results of your search, not on some dictionary-like thesaurus.

thrash

when you run out of hardware memory, an advanced operating system will free up memory space by moving the contents of some of your memory to disk. When that information is needed again, it is read from disk back into memory. When your computer is thrashing, memory is being swapped back and forth at such a rate that your hard drive is constantly spinning and not much else is happening with your computer.

thread

1. a series of postings on a particular topic. Threads can be a series of bulletin board messages (for example, when someone posts a question and others reply with answers or additional queries on the same topic). A thread can also apply to chats, where multiple conversation threads may exist simultaneously.
2. also refers to an independent process taking place in a multitasking environment.

three-beam projector

a computer/video projector having three colour beams (guns) to project computer and/or video images on the wall or large screens. These are generally the top of the line in terms of projection quality and lowest in line in terms of portability. Most of these have scan converters to convert computer RGB into NTSC images. Early models could only scan CGA images from PC computers. Modern versions can scan almost any type of computer display, although they may require skilled technicians to adjust the display whenever a computer is first connected to the projector. These projectors are very popular as ceiling mounts in electronic classrooms.

TIF

see **TIFF.**

TIFF

Tagged Image File Format. Graphics file format popularised by Aldus PageMaker for recognising graphics from different types of software. TIFF graphics files typically have a tif extension. see also **graphics**.

tiger video server

see **video server.**

tile

to automatically arrange windows in a tile-like configuration.

time line

a graphical representation of a span of time and the chronological relationship of events.

timeline presentation

a 'linear' presentation where the sequence on images or tasks is predetermined and cannot be interactively altered or modified by the user. This is just the opposite of 'non-linear' hypertext and hypermedia presentations where users interactively determine or partly determine the sequencing. see also **hypertext** and **hypermedia**.

title (of a document)

the official title of a document from the 'meta' field called title. The text of this meta title field may or may not also occur in the visible body of the document. It is what appears in the top bar of the window when you display the document and it is the title that appears in search engine results. The 'meta' field called title is not mandatory in HTML coding. Sometimes you retrieve a document with 'No Title' as its supposed title, this is caused when the meta-title field is left blank.

In Alta Vista and some other search tools, title: search also matches on the 'meta' field, which contains document descriptors not displayed on the Web.

title bar

the bar at the top of a window that displays the string of information about the item, usually a file name.

TLA

Three Letter Acronym.

TLD

Top Level Domain. The last (right-hand) part of a complete Domain Name. For example in the domain name www.matisse.net '.net' is the Top Level Domain.

There are a large number of TLD's, for example .biz, .com, .edu, .gov, .info, .int, .mil, .net, .org and a collection of two-letter TLD's corresponding to the standard two-letter country codes, for example, .us, .ca, .jp, etc.

TN3270

TN3270 is a special type of telnet that is sometimes needed to connect to IBM mainframe sites. Regular telnet will often work, but if you have trouble with keypresses and commands, you may need a tn3270 client to add to your software.

toggle

1. a switch that is either on or off.
2. if it is on, to turn it off, if it is off, to turn it on.

token

the data packet used to carry information on LANs using the ring topology.

token, authentication

hardware device that generates a one time password to authenticate its owner. Also sometimes applied to software programs that generate one time passwords.

toolbar

the row of buttons right below the menu that perform special functions quickly and easily.

toolbook

a Windows and Windows 2000 based authoring system for computer based training and education. The main competitor is Macromedia Authorware. ToolBook has full functionality with web delivery options of Neuron.

■ topology
the manner in which nodes are connected on a LAN.

■ TOS
acronym for 'The Other Service'. Often used among a group of people who have switched from one online service to another. The service they came from is 'the other service'. It often refers to Genie or AOL, but can refer to Compuserve or Prodigy or even the late NVN, depending on where a group originated.

■ tossed out
ejected from the chat rooms on America Online for violating its Terms of Service (TOS) agreement.

■ touchscreen
an overlay for a computer monitor screen that allows users to control navigation and other actions by touching the screen. Although widely used for children, touchscreens are also useful when customers enter reception areas and library users want to search holdings listings.

■ TPTB
acronym for 'The Powers That Be', refers to the management of the activity being discussed.

■ traceroute
an Internet utility that will show you the full connection path between your site and another Internet address. You can run your own traceroute software with a PPP or net connection. Windows 95, NT and beyond include a traceroute program (tracert.exe) which you can use from Start/ Run. First type command to call a DOS window. Then type the command tracert delphiforums.com (or any other address). NetLab is an excellent freeware program for Windows that includes traceroute and other utilities.

■ track-at-once recording
a mode that lets you record contents to a disk in multiple sessions, a track at a time.

■ traffic
the load of packets carried by a network or portion of a network. Heavy traffic slows down the response time of the individual packets.

■ transit spam
a form of e-mail spam which is sent through another Internet mail server than the one it originates from, usually with forged headers to make it look as if it originated from the through site, rather than the actual originating site.

■ transparent GIF
a type of GIF image where one colour, usually the background of the image, has been selected to appear as transparent. When placed on a web page, any background colour or tiled image will show through the transparency. It is the way to put graphics with shapes other than the usual rectangles on a page.

■ transport encryption

crypto services applied to information above the network level but below the application software level. This allows crypto protections to be applied to an existing application protocol and also use the existing network protocol stack and underlying networking services. Transport encryption is typically packaged with the application that it is protecting.

■ transport mode

ESP mode that encrypts the data contents of a packet and leaves the original IP addresses in plaintext.

■ triple des (3des)

cipher that applies the DES cipher three times with either two or three different DES keys.

■ triple-dub

an abbreviated way to say 'WWW' when reciting a URL.

■ trojan horse

a computer program is either hidden inside another program or that masquerades as something it is not in order to trick potential users into running it. For example a program that appears to be a game or image file but in reality performs some other function. The term 'Trojan Horse' comes from a possibly mythical ruse of war used by the Greeks sometime between 1500 and 1200 B.C.

A Trojan Horse computer program may spread itself by sending copies of itself from the host computer to other computers, but unlike a virus it will (usually) not infect other programs.

■ troll

an outrageous message posted to a newsgroup or mailing list or message board to bait people to answer. Trolling is a form of harassment that can take over a discussion. Well meaning defenders can create chaos by responding to trolls. The best response is to ignore it. Also, the person who posts such messages.

■ trumpet winsock

a popular, cheerier TCP/IP protocol stack.

■ truncation

in a search, the ability to enter the first part of a keyword, insert a symbol (usually *) and accept any variant spellings or word endings, from the occurrence of the symbol forward. (E.g., femini* retrieves feminine, feminism, feminism, etc.)

■ trustee rights

rights given to users to access directories on the file server.

■ TTFN

chat shorthand for 'Ta Ta For Now'.

■ tunnel mode

ESP mode that encrypts an entire IP packet including the IP header.

■ tweak

to make many minor adjustments. To fine tune. Also, a minor adjustment.

■ twisted pair

a twisted pair is a pair of insulated wires that twist around each other repeatedly in a spiral pattern along the length of the wires. Twisting them rather than running them side by side reduces electromagnetic interference. Ordinary telephone cable in the house usually consists of two or three twisted pairs, with each wire coded in a different colour insulation. Twisted pairs surrounded by a shielding ground layer are known as shielded twisted pair. Twisted pair is often used in Ethernet LANs.

■ UDP

User Datagram Protocol. **O**ne of the protocols for data transfer that is part of the TCP/IP suite of protocols. UDP is a 'stateless' protocol in that UDP makes no provision for acknowledgement of packets received.

■ ultimedia video

is IBM Corporation's OS/2 equivalent of Video for Windows. Ultimedia Video IN/2 is priced at under $200 and supports video capture and editing in IBM Ultimation and Indeo compression formats. It can deliver up to 30 fps at 320 by 240 window size if the user's hardware can handle the upper-end capabilities.

■ UML

Uniform Modelling Language. When people initially get down to work with the Unified Modelling Language (UML), it is typically the first time they take up the practice of use cases. These are an important element of UML, intended to help gather functional requirements, as well as to provide a means of communication among development team members. But use cases are not without controversy. And for long-time industry observers, the controversy may be somewhat familiar. Many of the brickbats loosed years ago upon Case tools and structural analysis are now aimed at UML and use cases. Use cases lead to 'analysis paralysis.' Use cases are 'shelfware'. These are just some of the criticisms unloaded by influential software consultants and authors, many of whom are counted among the ranks of eXtreme Programming (XP) advocates.

At times, the XP squad, although it includes a number of individuals who see some merit in use cases, seems to echo the arguments of Rapid Application Development (RAD) advocates of the client/server era. These earlier RAD advocates challenged development orthodoxy of the day, which centred on 'waterfall' processes. The RAD folk also took some arrows for creating a few allegedly non-scalable and non-repeatable systems.

On one level, the battle—and 'battle' is probably too powerful a word—between UML and XP is new evidence of the timeless divide between designers who want just a little more time to do a little more analysis of system needs and developers who just want to start coding.

This situation is natural. UML had something of a honeymoon. It arose in the late 1990s out of the combined efforts of notable software methodologists Grady Booch, James Rumbaugh and Ivar Jacobson, who came to work at Rational Software Corp. and who came to be known in a series of road shows as 'The Three Amigos'. The battle of the object methodologies was effectively ended as UML standardisation responsibility was eventually ceded to the Object Management Group (OMG). Now, as UML is increasingly used, developers have had some mixed experiences, so there is a higher likelihood that UML will take a few shots.

While the recent UML World 2001 conference held in New York City featured sessions that considered new UML extensions and studied best practices in UML use case gathering, the conference was just as notable for a use case panel at which UML and XP proponents traded verbal barbs.

Focus on the guerre du jour, this effort will instead uncover some user experiences with use cases. This will hopefully provide a useful backdrop for development managers trying to visualise their next steps in design and development.

■ unencod/undecode

see **Internet messaging.**

■ unicode

like ASCII, Unicode is a code which assigns a number to each key on the keyboard. Unicode is newer and includes many characters not found in ASCII such as international characters and alphabets.

■ Uniform Resource Identifier (URI)

see **RDF**.

■ Uniform Resource Locator (URL)

an addressing scheme used by World Wide Web browsers to locate resources on the Internet.

■ Uninterruptible Power Supply (UPS)

a device that keeps computers running after a power failure, providing power from batteries for a short period of time.

■ unique visitor

a real visitor to a web site. Web servers record the IP addresses of each visitor and this is used to determine the number of real people who have visited a web site. If, for example, someone visits twenty pages within a web site, the server will count only one unique visitor (because the page accesses are all associated with the same IP address) but twenty page accesses.

see also **hit** and **page view**.

UNIX

an operating system developed by Bell Laboratories for use on large workstations. Latest information on Copeland and other operating systems can be obtained at <http://techweb.cmp.com/iw/center/default.html>. UNIX became one of the main operating systems for networked computers. It is especially suited for networks and is commonly used for Internet networks. The UNIX System V Release 4 based operating system is called Sun's Solaris that runs off Sun Workstations and the PowerPC. IBM's Unix-based operating system is called the AIX and the Hewlett-Packard version is called HP/UX. A discussion of whether Unix should become more of a part of operating systems in accounting practices is provided by Courtney and Hunton (1993). Since the advent of Windows 2000, much of this argument becomes muted.

As the Windows platform continues to evolve to address changing business computing needs, many organisations currently on UNIX platforms are turning to Windows to run their new client and server business applications. They're discovering that moving to the Windows platform does not require abandoning existing investments in UNIX applications and infrastructure.

Unlicensed National Information Infrastructure (U-NII) band

an unregulated radio frequency that uses the 5 GHz band for communication. This band is divided into three sub-bands and are intended for use by short-range, high-speed wireless digital communication devices.

upload

to transfer a file from your computer system to another system via a modem over telephone or cable lines or a telnet connection using a transfer protocol like xmodem, ymodem, zmodem or Kermit. Less precisely, it may also refer to a direct transfer from your local terminal to a server over a local area network or an FTP transfer from your system to a remote system. see **download**.

urban legend

an oft-told tale on the Internet that is untrue, but refuses to die. They keep reappearing in newsgroups, e-mail discussion lists and message bases. The stories themselves are interesting and when newcomers read them for the first time, they are often passed along as fact. They may have been once true as in the Craig Shergold get-well card story, a hoax like the GOOD TIMES VIRUS or a joke, like the expensive Neiman-Marcus cookie recipe. They often appear with variations,.so that get-well cards become business cards or Neiman-Marcus becomes Mrs. Fields instead.

■ URI

Universal Resource Identifier. A standardised method of identifying and locating resources which includes Uniform Resource Names (URN) and Uniform Resource Locators (URL). The system is only partly implemented today, but when fully implemented, when a URN is requested, it will be systematically matched with a set of URLs for the resource to find the best available route to the resource.

■ URN

Uniform Resource Name. A URI that is supposed to be available for along time. For an address to be a URN some institution is supposed to make a commitment to keep the resource available at that address.

■ Usenet Newsgroups

Usenet Newsgroups are discussion groups about a topic that is reflected in their titles, such as comp.sys.ibm.pc.games.adventure or sci.astro.hubble. Many of the newsgroups have worldwide distribution and their followers post messages, properly called 'articles', for all to read and respond to. The 'Usenet' part of the title refers to their distribution via the unix to unix network. Strictly speaking, newsgroups are a Usenet, not an Internet protocol, but they are widely picked up by Internet providers. There are eight major primary series of newsgroups: comp, humanities, misc, news, rec, sci, soc and talk. Newsgroups in the eight primary series are only created after a formal approval process, which includes formal discussion and voting. In addition, there are less formal alternative newsgroups with the alt series the primary one and many others with a regional or local focus such as the nyc series or the uk series or topics with limited distribution and purpose like k12 or fedreg. To participate in newsgroups, you should learn the purpose and the norms of the newsgroup before posting any articles of your own. A good rule of thumb is to read for two weeks before posting and then follow the norms. Many newsgroups post a FAQ: Frequently Asked Questions file about once a month, which you should look at before posting for the first time.

■ user

a person who uses computer software or hardware as opposed to someone who develops computer software or hardware. Sometimes used in a diminutive sense as in 'I can't believe how brain-dead our users are'.

■ user app

see **plug-in.**

■ user ID

the name by which you are identified by a particular network. In order to log onto a system, you need to supply both a user ID and a password.

utility

a small computer program that performs some very useful function. For example, utilities exist to convert files from one format to another, to compress files, to detect and eliminate viruses and to defragment hard drives. Utilities fill the gaps in an operating system, providing useful features that were left out. As an operating system grows, it often incorporates the features that were previously delivered only by utilities.

UUCP

abbreviation for Unix-to-Unix Copy. UNIX software that allows e-mail and news messages to be exchanged on a store-and-forward basis between remote computers. Before the rise of the Internet, this was the main way that remote UNIX machines were networked. It is no longer in wide use.

VAP

a Value-Added Process to the NetWare operation system provided by a third party vendor.

variable

a named container that holds values, either numeric or text.

VCR

a videotape player designed to connect to television sets or computer video capture boards. Videotapes are recorded in video format (e.g., NTSC or PAL) in half, three quarter or one inch formats. The most common tape is the half-inch VHS tape, but for professional video materials and videodisc mastering one-inch tape is preferred. see also **VHS**, **Video** and **Videodisc.**

vector graphics

in mathematics and physics, a vector is a line which has a defined starting point, a designated direction and a specified distance. Vector graphics are line-based graphics. In vector graphics, vectors determine how straight and curved lines (Beziers or splines) are shaped between specific points. The lines and the colours of areas enclosed by the lines make up the picture. Microsoft SYLK is an example of a pure vector format. More commonly used are bitmap files and hybrids of vector and bitmap known as metafiles.

venona

U.S. military project to cryptanalyse Soviet one time pad ciphertext from the 1940s.

vernam cipher

Cipher developed for encrypting teletype traffic by computing the exclusive or of the data bits and the key bits. This is a common approach for constructing stream ciphers.

veronica

the gopher-based search engine that worked with an index of gopher menus around the world. The last Veronica search engine on the nets is probably gone for good, but before the web's spectacular growth, it was a real workhorse for searchers . It supposedly is an acronym for Very Easy Rodent-Oriented Netwide Index to Computerised Archives, but since the archie FTP search preceded it in time, the name pretty obviously came before the acronym.

VHS

videotape having 240-325 lines of horizontal resolution. Super VHS (S-VHS) and videodiscs contain up to 425 lines of resolution. S-VHS tape decks can also play VHS formats. see also **Video**.

video

a term that was once used to refer almost exclusively to analog recordings of images on tape that can be replayed at 30 or more frames per second (fps) depicting 'full motion video'. Since the age of digitisation, the term now refers to analog or digital recordings (e.g., digitised video in computer files and HDTV) that can be replayed at 30 fps or a reasonably close approximation of full motion video. The term differs somewhat from 'animation' in that animations are successions of still frames not necessarily intended to be 'full-motion' at speeds comparable to video full motion. The highest quality video connectors are termed S-video connectors, whereas the lowest quality connector is the RF connector. Because of the tremendous bandwidth required for network transmission of video between computers, it is not yet common to watch a movie on the Internet. The wave of the future is MPEG compression. However, until there are millions of computer users with enough computer hardware capacity to run MPEG digitised video, Microsoft Video for Windows and Apple QuickTime will probably remain more common in CD-ROM authoring of education materials. Video options for the PC with particular stress upon Intel's Indeo Video and Smart Video Recorder are analysed.

video adapter

the video hardware that determines the resolution and colour depth of screen images. A k-bit adapter can display 2 to the kth power colours. For example, an 8-bit adapter displays up to 256 colours whereas a 24-bit adapter can display over 16 millions colours in a single screen. In hypermedia authoring, problems are created when the colour depth of the authored image is higher than the colour depth of the user (customer, student, reader) computer. Mac and PowerPC computers will usually dither to make the image reasonably good for users, whereas PC users may have terrible images if their video adapters are too low in colour depth. The same thing can happen if the user's PC screen resolution adapter is lower than the authored PC screen. These are terribly frustrating problems for authors and users. For this reason, most of the commercial PC graphics and video CD-ROM files are authored for lower video adapters than the author's video adapter. For example, the author may be capable of presenting a graphics image in 30 million colours in a resolution of 1024 by 768. The author may elect, however, to only use no more than 256 colours in standard VGA resolution in order to have better images on user computers with lower powered video adapters.

■ video board

a somewhat misleading term that can apply to video capture and/or video playback hardware inside a computer. Video can be played back on computers without having video capture hardware. This enables CD-ROM users to view video and animations without having to install MPC or other standard video capture boards. However, if video capture boards are installed, users can also connect their computers to video sources (video recorders, video cameras and television signals) in order to either view incoming video 'on the fly' and/or capture segments of the video into digitised formats such as quick time, AVI, MPEG or JPEG video formats. Video files should not be saved using disk compression utilities like Doublespace or Stacker. For capturing and playback of digitised video into and out of computer files, a full-motion video frame grabber (digitiser) of some type allows authors to capture selected full-motion video (camcorder, videotape, videodisc, cable TV, satellite dish, etc.) images and convert those analog frames into digital graphics files on the computer. Video boards (cards) and frame grabbers start at around $200, but prices vary a great deal with vendors and options, including options under Microsoft Windows Video MCI standards, Apple QuickTime standards, IBM M-Motion (MM) standards, MPEG standards and Intel Indeo standards. Virtually every major computer brand on the market has multiple options for video (multimedia) devices. Many of those devices also have accompanying frame grabber software. For example, readers may consider Pioneer's LaserActive system (213-746-6337). Compression boards for PCs come in a variety of prices and features. MPEG compression requires MPEG playback boards and/or MPEG authoring boards such as the Optibase MPG-1000 digital video code compression/decompression) board (800-451-5101). However, until there are millions of computer users with newer computer hardware capacity to run MPEG digitized video, Microsoft Video for Windows under MCI standards and Apple QuickTime will probably remain more common in CD-ROM authoring of education materials until the market sorts out its preferences for MPEG, DVI and the Intel Indeo. The term 'video overlay' is used to depict a video board option to view live video 'on the fly' in a monitor screen without burdening the CPU until the user elects to capture video. Not all video cards have video overlay options.

video camera

a camcorder camera that records full-motion images and audio directly to videotape. Video cameras exist for filming tapes of varying widths. Usually the wider the tape (e.g. one inch versus half inch), the better the picture quality. However, other factors such as High 8 versus Regular 8 come into play. High 8 cameras are especially popular among hand-held cameras, because of the professional quality for the size and price of the camera. Users who, for example, purchase an 8 mm video camera can play the tape into a videotape recorder and record VHS tapes or videotapes of other widths.

video capture

a process of transforming a video (e.g., NTSC) image into a computer (digitised) image. Video capturing options are reviewed in a famous magazine. The process entails adding hardware and software designed to transform an analog (TV) image, say from a videotape, into a digital computer image. Usually a video capture board must be installed that is compatible with the bus of the computer. For example, a PC generally has an ISA, EISA or MCA bus that in turn requires a compatible video capture board inside the computer. Video boards also enable computer users to view videotape or television images 'on-the-fly' without necessarily capturing the images into computer files. Video capture boards vary greatly in price and quality. What is best for a given computer depends a great deal upon the amount of RAM, video RAM, graphics adapter, screen resolution, colour depth and speed of the computer.

video for windows

animation and video files that originally were developed by Microsoft Corporation for PCs running under Windows. This has become a widely popular option for PCs operating under MCI standards. Like QuickTime, Video for Windows is a low cost and low fps option that will be common in CD-ROM authoring of education materials until MPEG compression options and video networking become more widespread. Although Microsoft's Video for Windows and Apple's QuickTime captured early market share leads in digital video, newer and better compression alternatives such as

Indeo and MPEG probably will take over this market.

video server

the combination of hardware and software that allows for storage and transmission of continuous animation and video in real time. The core of a video server is a continuous media operating system that allows animation, audio and real-time video to be processed and transmitted across networks or over digital television satellites. Major players are rushing to develop video servers, including the over $100 million dollar per year effort by the Advanced Technology Group (ATG) and Microsoft Corporation to develop the Tiger video server as part of the overall information highway architecture development code named Mimosa by Microsoft managers.

video streaming

see **web streaming.**

video/audio networking (streaming)

refers to audio and video on network that commences to play before files are fully downloaded. The terms 'real' and 'streaming' are synonyms in terms of network video and audio.

videoconferencing

remote communication in which two-way video images are transmitted with audio. Although this can be accomplished with video cameras on special telephone connections, it is now possible to become much more sophisticated with videoconferencing using computers. Purportedly, the highest proportion of videoconferencing worldwide is for education and training.

videodisc

an antiquated 'large' (more than 12 cm or 4.72 inches) injection-moulded optical disc containing digitised information that has been recorded with a laser device and must be read on a laser device known as a videodisc player. The most common sizes are eight and 12-inch discs. A 12-inch disc will hold 54,000 video frames of super VHS quality. Full-length movies usually require more than one disc since only 30 minutes of video with audio can be stored on each side of a 12-inch CAV disc. A CLV disc can hold up to 60 minutes per side of a 12-inch disc. CLV holds more video but is more limited than CAV in terms of searching for individual frames. Two audio tracks can accompany a video track, thereby enabling educational audio to accompany entertainment audio. Although a videodisc resembles a CD-ROM in appearance, there are major differences. Relative to a CD-ROM disc, the laser disc is 'large' in varying sizes of eight or more inches. Whereas a CD-ROM player can hold computer files and computer graphics images in common file extensions (e.g., GIF, BMP, PCX, TIF, JPG, etc.) and can be treated as a computer storage disc somewhat analogous to a high-capacity floppy disc, a videodisc cannot hold computer files. Videodiscs are more like videotape in that they are recorded in video formats such as NTSC or PAL or SECAM. Videodisc players are generally connected to television sets and will play on-the-fly in a computer only if that computer has a video board for any video source such as television inputs and VCR inputs. Videodisc and videotape images can be 'captured' and transformed into computer files only if the computer has video capture hardware and software. Videodiscs are currently used in some multimedia presentations but their future in hypermedia is uncertain. Videodisc players cannot be made portable as CD-ROM players. Recently options became available for desktop recording of videodiscs. For example, Panasonic (201-348-7837) offers the LQ-3031T model starting at $12,500. However, most videodiscs mastered in professional labs require inputs of professional-quality videotape (usually one-inch videotape) produced in a video workstation. A second drawback of videodiscs is that, unlike CD-ROM discs, videodiscs cannot be previewed prior to being mastered. There are two types of videodiscs known as CAV and CLV. The most common entertainment and educational videodiscs are CLV discs. There are currently four levels of interactivity for videodisc players. Level 'one' is controlled with an infrared or wired remote control or bar code reader. Level 'two' players have programmable memory. Level 'three' is controlled by an external computer which greatly improves interactive controls with hypermedia software. Level 'four' is a high speed computer interface videodisc player that accesses each side of the videodisc. Level four is more useful for using a videodisc as an external storage device for computer data.

■ **videodisc levels**

see **videodisc.**

■ **videodisc-digital**

a videodisc in digital format. For example, the DDV-7100 8-bit, 4.5 MHz bandwidth model was unveiled in October 1993 by Optical Disc Corporation (800-350-3500). The DDV-7100 will hold four hours of compressed digital video on one side of a 12-inch videodisc. Later systems will hold up to 10 gigabytes of data or one hour of HDTV. This technology is intended for interactive television of the future and for satellite uplinks and mass storage video servers. Playback units start at under $5,000 but recording units are likely to be found only in professional videodisc recording and reproduction laboratories since the disc recorder sells for almost $100,000 and requires other workstation hardware and software. This technology will probably be overtaken by newer CD-DVD technology.

■ virtual

a seeming reality that lacks some elements of total reality. Since the early days of computing, simulation has become the most common form of achieving virtual worlds for learning and research. The term 'virtual' is now loosely applied in many contexts. At one extreme it is applied to almost anything connected with a computer or networks. For example, network chat lines may be viewed as 'virtual communities'. Interactive creation (by multiple persons) of artificial worlds (e.g., MUDs, MOOs, MUSHes, simulations, etc.) has become a major component in creating virtual communities. At the other extreme there is virtual reality in its most advanced stages with headgear, wired body suits, simulated odours, simulated tactile sensations, surrounding 3-D worlds, interactions of multiple people and machines in a shared cyberspace, etc. Entire courses are either using or devoting the course to 'virtual communities'. For example, students in a sociology course at Northern Arizona University create virtual communities in a simulation of the colonisation of Mars. The term 'virtual community' has evolved to where it usually refers to 'conversations' that are not face-to-face and are often anonymous to at least the point where speakers cannot be identified (although groups to which they belong might be known). The key element is anonymity. Corporate boards of directors and other groups often pay to rent 'silent meeting rooms' that are available in some universities such as the University of Arizona, Syracuse University, the University of Wisconsin at Milwaukee and other campuses. In a '**silent meeting**,' participants can be face-to-face and still communicate anonymously. This is because the 'conversations' are taking place within the computers in front of all participants. When a participant makes a point, none of the other participants can detect which person in the room made the comment.

■ virtual domain

a domain hosted by a virtual server account.

■ Virtual Private Network (VPN)

a private network within a public network, usually on the Internet. Privacy for the virtual network is achieved through encryption and provides a less expensive option than using dedicated lines.

virtual reality

a computer simulation of a real 3-dimensional world, often supplemented by sound effects. One early example allowed you to drive through a city, turn at any street intersection and see what you would see out of a car window. Another let you learn a ship's layout by moving throughout all of its decks. Modern games let you fly an airplane or spaceship in combat or explore a dungeon and kill its monsters. Educational applications let you learn through experience for many types of simulated tasks or interact with professors and class members at a distance. See **VRML**.

Virtual Reality Markup Language (VRML)

a scripting language used to define three-dimensional 'worlds'.

virtual server

an account on a hosting company server, usually linked to its own domain. This provides an inexpensive way to run a web site with its own top level domain and is usually indistinguishable from having a separate physical server, except that the virtual server may share an IP address with other virtual servers on the same machine. A virtual server account is fine for most uses, but will often be slower to respond than a physically separate server and physical access to the machine will seldom be allowed. The cost of a virtual server account is a small fraction of that needed to run a real server, mainly because of the expense of the dedicated line needed to connect the server continuously to the rest of the net.

virtual-image file

a set of pointers to the files on your hard disk to be sent to the CD-R drive, rather than a duplicate physical-image of those files. Usually employed for on-the-fly recording.

virus

a chunk of computer programming code that makes copies of itself without any conscious human intervention. Some viruses do more than simply replicate themselves, they might display messages, install other software or files, delete software of files, etc. A virus requires the presence of some other program to replicate itself. Typically viruses spread by attaching themselves to programs and in some cases files, for example the file formats for Microsoft word processor and spreadsheet programs allow the inclusion of programs called 'macros' which can in some cases be a breeding ground for viruses.

Visual Basic (VB)

an extension of Microsoft Basic that allows for GUI controls, animations and drag-and-drop features. Its main competitors are Borland's Delphi and Sun's Java. VB is used in many Microsoft products and in numerous applications by third parties. The main web site for Visual Basic at Microsoft is http://www.microsoft.com/vbasic/. VBX is a Visual Basic custom control used in may software components. VBX components allow developers to more quickly write Visual Basic components. When used in conjunction with Windows Scripting Host utilities, Visual Basic adds great risks for viruses when using e-mail and web browsing software from Microsoft. For more discussion of such matters, see **ActiveX**.

■ Vl-bus

a local bus standard set by the Video Electronics Standards Association (VESA) that requires direct-to-CPU connections that limit the number of expansion slots in computers. The VL-Bus is faster than EISA and less expensive to manufacture. For a time it was the bus of choice for PCs until the newer PCI bus was introduced by Intel.

■ voice recognition

see **speech recognition.**

■ vortal

a vertical portal. A specialised portal that serves a particular organisation or interest group, rather than trying to be all things to all people.

■ VR

see **Virtual Reality.**

■ VRAM

Video Random Access Memory. Chips that determine the performance capacity of video adapter hardware in computers. In particular, they allow for reading and writing of graphics images to take place simultaneously. At the time of this writing, authors of hypermedia are advised to purchase a computer with at least 2Mb of VRAM.

■ VRML

Virtual Reality Modelling Language. A graphical system that creates views of 3-dimensional images that change as the viewer's angle and position changes and light sources change. It can be used to create an environment or world that appears realistic as you 'move' through it. It is widely used for games and for educational applications. The technology is very young and growing fast. It requires a fast computer and fast video support with lots of memory to be effective.

■ W3C

abbreviation for the World Wide Web Consortium, the organisation that develops standards for the web community.

■ WAIS

Wide Area Information Servers. A commercial software package that allows the indexing of huge quantities of information and then making those indices searchable across networks such as the Internet . A prominent feature of WAIS is that the search results are ranked according to how relevant the 'hits' are and that subsequent searches can find 'more stuff like that last batch' and thus refine the search process.

■ WAIS gateway

this term refers to a computer that is used to translate WAIS data so it can be made available to an otherwise incompatible network or application. Mosaic must use a WAIS gateway.

■ WAN

stands for Wide Area Network. A network of computers that covers a large geographical distance.

■ wannabee

a would-be hacker.

■ WAP

Wireless Application Protocol. A protocol used with small handheld devices with small file sizes.

■ warez

software pirated by dOoDz (immature scofflaws).

■ watermark

a background image in HTML documents that does not scroll like larger images that are not watermarks. For example, in the Microsoft FrontPage Editor, if you click on Page Properties and Background, one of the options is to import a watermark image for your web page.

■ wav file

a wav file format used by Microsoft Windows for storing digitised audio. All information necessary to generate voice and music is stored in the file. MP3 is a file format which stores audio files on a computer in such a way that the file size is relatively small, but the song sounds near perfect. You can identify MP3 files because they will end in MP3. Typically 1 MB is equal to one minute of music or several minutes for spoken work/audiobooks. This is about a 90% reduction in hard drive space and bandwidth vis-à-vis uncompressed high quality wav files, but the actual savings depends upon the recording quality of your wav files. If you think about a CD-ROM holding 650 Mb, this translates to over 11 hours of high quality audio in MP3 format. More importantly, MP3 audio does not require as much Internet bandwidth as previous audio alternatives.

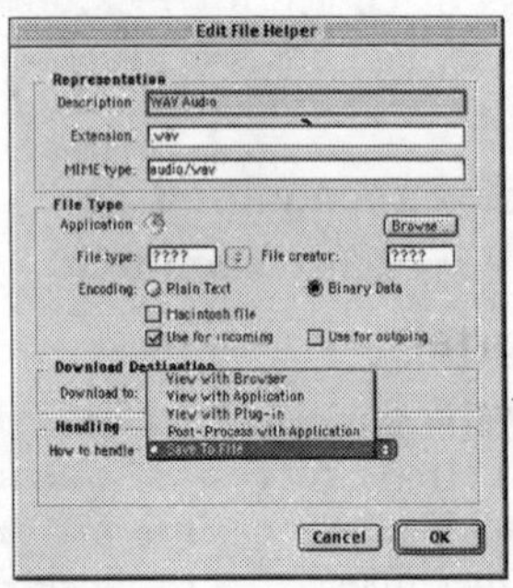

■ web

short for 'World Wide Web'.

■ web browsers

interfaces to the World Wide Web that simplify locating web pages, downloading files, playing of audio, playing of video, etc. Gopher was the first to become a great hit, but it was limited mainly to text. Mosaic followed, but it was Netscape that hit the market with enormous success. Netscape Navigator can be downloaded from <http://www.netscape.com/. This success jolted Microsoft into expanding its network browser development from six employees to more than 600 developers. The Microsoft browser is known as Explorer (see <http://www.microsoft.com/>). Various other competitors are emerging, but it is a market share browser race between Netscape Navigator and Explorer. Features to both are added almost monthly, so it is very difficult to stay up to date on the latest happenings without going directly to the vendor web pages. Most browser vendors also sell software for creating and maintaining web (home) pages. Students can set up free homepages at <http://www.tripod.com/>. Virtual Servers Inc., for a monthly fee, will provide web server space to business firms and other parties wanting to set up network application servers. The Virtual Server home page is http://vservers.com/. In the past, browsing was free of virus risks. With the advent of Windows Scripting Host utilities, this is no longer the case. Precautionary advice is given under ActiveX.

Windows users mostly prefer Internet Explorer that comes bundled in Microsoft Office. A key advantage of Internet Explorer is that it supports DHTML dynamic Webpages. Another advantage is that it now supports XML and XBRL.

■ web copywriting

the writing of text especially for a web page. Similar to the writing of copy for any other type of publication, good web copywriting can have a great effect on search engine positioning, so it forms a major part of optimisation.

■ web document

an HTML document, Gopher document, a PDF document or some other document that is browsable on the Internet.

■ web node

this term is synonymous with Web site or Web server.

■ web page

a document designed for viewing in a web browser. Typically written in HTML. A web site is made of one or more web pages.

■ web streaming

live playback of media files on the web. The most common way to execute media files (audio and video) is to download those files into a local computer and then launch a plug-in or applications program to execute the media file in question. Users have an option of saving the files, although the usual default condition is only to store the file temporarily. Web streaming is quite different. In that case, audio or video files play in real time without having to wait for full downloads of the files. In general, web streaming playback is of lower quality than download playback, but streaming avoids downloading interruptions and the need for storage space in a local computer. However, these are not mutually exclusive options. Streaming can actually be in real time or in 'pseudo' web streams. Pseudo streaming downloads a portion of a file sufficient to play it back in somewhat better quality than real time streaming on the fly. Some pseudo streaming software require beginning at the start of the file while others allow starting at various points in the file. MIDI technology is on the rise for audio web streaming.

■ web surfing

browsing the WWW using a Web browser. Users search for information, chat lines, business transactions and many other purposes. Surfing generally refers to the 'pull' approach where the user pulls in the fish. Casting (webcasting, netcasting, Castanet, etc.) generally refers to the 'push' approach where the user selects channels for preferred types of information and then lets the channel push updates automatically into the user's computer. In the past, web surfing was free of virus risks. With the advent of Windows Scripting Host utilities, this is no longer the case. Precautionary advice is given under ActiveX. see also **Internet**, **search engine**, **webcasting**, **world wide web and web surfing**.

■ web surfing backwards

once you have your web documents up and running, you may want to learn more about who is using these documents.

■ webcasting

use of World Wide Web to broadcast information. Unlike typical surfing, which relies on a pull method of transferring web pages, webcasting uses a 'push' combination of technologies to send information to users' computers. This is also referred to as 'broadcasting, channel surfing or 'netcasting'. Users get steady updates of streams of information in requested categories. Users can subscribe to a 'channel', download software to a local computer and then streams of automatic updates follow. The most popular webcasting service to date is PointCast, but several major companies, including Microsoft and Netscape, have announced their own webcasting products and services. For example Netscape announced it 'Netscape Netcaster' as follows:

Netscape Netcaster, the newest component of Netscape Communicator, enables push delivery of information and offline browsing. Netcaster seamlessly integrates with Channel Finder, the source for the best channels on the Internet. Users can subscribe to the information they want and have it delivered automatically. Offline browsing allows users to take the valuable resources of the Web offline with them - wherever they go. Developed entirely using the open Internet standards of HTML, Java and JavaScript, Netscape Netcaster is an example of the powerful applications that can be built on the Netscape ONE platform.

Microsoft's Channel Definition Format (CDF) used in 'Web Push Channels' and Netscape's Meta Content Framework (MCF) preceeded RDF. These technologies describe information resources in a manner somewhat similar to RDF and can be used to filter web sites and web documents such as filtering pornography and violence. They can be used to channel inflows of desired or undesired web information. CDF, for example, carries information not read on computer screens that perform metadata tasks. See **Resource Description Format (RDF) and search engine.**

■ webcrawler

one of the largest search engines. The URL is http://www.webcrawler.com.

■ webledger

an online accounting system in which a vendor of accounting services (e.g., bookkeeping, receivables management, bill paying, inventory management, financial statement preparation and tax services) are provided to multiple firms by a WebLedger vendor.

■ webliography

a listing of source World Wide Web sites.

■ Weblog (blog)

a Weblog (which is sometimes written as 'web log' or 'weblog') is a Web site of personal or non-commercial origin that uses a dated log format that is updated on a daily or very frequent basis with new information about a particular subject or range of subjects. The information can be written by the site owner, gleaned from other Web sites or other sources or contributed by users. A Web log often has the quality of being a kind of 'log of our times' from a particular point-of-view. Generally, Weblogs are devoted to one or several subjects or the mes, usually of topical interest and, in general, can be thought of as developing commentaries, individual or collective on their particular themes. A Weblog may consist of the recorded ideas of an individual (a sort of diary) or be a complex collaboration open to anyone. It's been said that newspapers write the first draft of history, but now there are blogs.

Weblogs continue to grow in popularity, no doubt in part to their immediacy. Denizens of the Internet enjoy the opportunity to drop by and catch an up-to-the-minute account on their favourite blog. However, nothing is more frustrating than encountering a cobwebbed blog that hasn't been updated in weeks. To remedy such situations, this site offers a minute-by-minute account of over 50,000 weblogs. It doesn't get fresher than this! For utility's sake, the site offers a tiny java applet that sits on your desktop and continually refreshes, keeping the weblogs whirring. You can also stop by the most popular blogs to see what kind of content is piquing the interest of others. Whether you're a neophyte or veteran blogger, you're sure to find an intriguing site or two to scour.

A blog is an easily updated Web site that works as an online day-book, consisting of links to interesting items on the Web, spur-of-the-moment observations and real-time reports on whatever captures the blogger's attention.

■ webmaster

this term refers to the person in charge of administrating a World Wide Web site.

■ website

the entire collection of *web pages* and other information (such as images, sound and video files, etc.) that are made available through what appears to users as a single web server. Typically all the of pages in a web site share the same basic *URL*, for example the following URLs are all for pages within the same web site:

http://www.baytherapy.com/
http://www.baytherapy.com/whatis/
http://www.baytherapy.com/teenagers/

The term has a somewhat informal nature since a large organisation might have separate 'web sites' for each division, but someone might talk informally about the organisations' 'web site' when speaking of all of them.

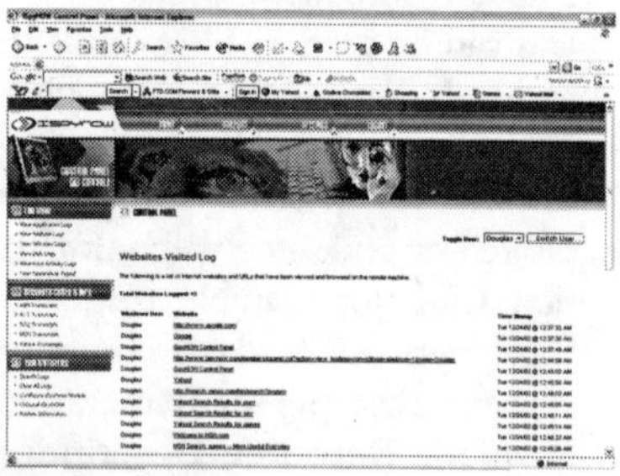

■ webspace

this term refers to the space created by the World Wide Web.

■ webtag

a term unique to Delphi Forums which designates a particular Forum on that service. Every Forum has its own webtag, different from all others, which forms part of the address for web pages, message boards and chat rooms for that Forum. Addresses take these forms:
Main web page: http://forums.delphiforums.com/webtag/

Start page: http://forums.delphiforums.com/webtag/start
Message board: http://forums.delphiforums.com/webtag/messages
Chat room: http://forums.delphiforums.com/webtag/chat
Replace 'webtag' with the actual webtag to link to the appropriate place. If you are linking to the web page, message board or chat room, use the appropriate anchor tag, which will be one of these:
<a href='http://forums.delphiforums.com/webtag/'> WebPageName</a>
<a href='http://forums.delphiforums.com/webtag/start'> WebPageName Start Page</a>
<a href='http://forums.delphiforums.com/webtag/messages'> WebPageName Message Board</a>
<a href='http://forums.delphiforums.com/webtag/chat'> WebPageName Chat</a:>

■ WebTV

a way of accessing Internet and e-mail service via a set-top box, a television set, a standard phone line and a subscription-based online service called WebTV Network. WebTV is a failure is the opinion of one professional who writes in a famous magazine.

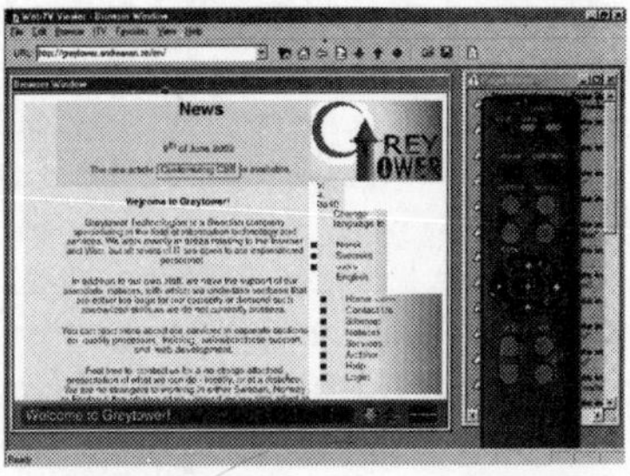

■ WEP

Wired Equivalent Privacy or less frequently, Wireless Encryption Protocol. A security protocol for wireless networks defined in the 802.11b standard. Being keyphrase based, it does not provide a high enough level of security for critical data that might be specifically targeted for its value, but is reasonable for home network security in most cases.

■ wetware

hacker slang for the human central nervous system, especially the brain. Most computing systems have three essential components: software, hardware and wetware.

■ WHOIS

an Internet utility that you can use to look up information about an Internet site in the registry database at Internic or elsewhere. You can enter a name like Delphi, a domain address like delphiforums.com or a full or partial IP address and get information on the site's name, address, points of contact, etc. The utility can be run with your own ISP or net account or you can use the

Network Solutions Whois web page for domain names and the American Registry of Internet Numbers (ARIN) for IP addresses. There are also WHOIS servers in Europe (RIPE), Australia and Asia-Pacific Network Information Centre (APNIC). Many more WHOIS servers are maintained for particular organisations. A very complete list of Internet WHOIS servers is kept at MIT. NetLab is an excellent Win 95 freeware program that includes whois and other utilities. WS-FTP Pro, an excellent shareware FTP program, also provides whois and other utilities in its package.

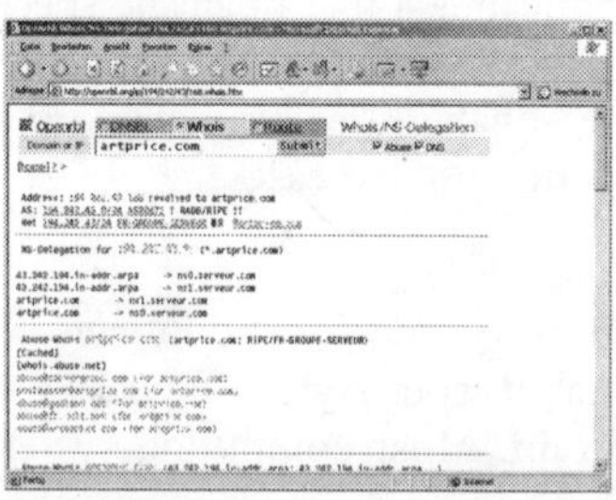

WHOIS gateway

a source listing of e-mail addresses around the world on the Internet. see also **Mosaic.**

wide-screen TV

television sets with a 16:9 movie theatre aspect ratio for home theatre systems. Standard broadcast aspect ratios are 4:3. The W-VHS is a wide-screen HDTV recorder and tape deck introduced by JVC in Japan that will record the Japanese version of HDTV as well as standard TV signals.

Wi-Fi

Wireless Fidelity. A popular term for a form of wireless data communication, basically Wi-Fi is 'Wireless Ethernet'.

window

an old term for a framed active area displayed on a bit-mapped computer display.

Windows

a windowing (Mac-like) extended DOS operating system from Microsoft Corporation that allows users to have more than one application running at the same time. Because Windows ran on lower-capacity 386 and 486 chips, it captured huge market shares and had over 40 million adopters by the end of 1993. This has severely clouded the future of Apple Corporation whose graphical operating system lost its uniqueness and popularity as Windows operating systems spread across the world. Windows applications can be stacked in succeeding 'windows' that have menu lines and, unlike Mac processors, have an ability to 'minimise' multiple operating programs. Users can then dart back and forth between windows (applications) without having to reload. Popular windows programs include those on Macintosh computers and on PCs using Microsoft Windows, Works and Enable. Finder is another windows program. It has become common for the word 'Windows' in computer lore to refer to Microsoft Windows built upon the DOS foundation. Newer OS/2 and Windows 2000 (New Technology) shed the DOS foundation but require considerably greater hardware capacity than the older Microsoft Windows.

■ Windows 2000

the updated name for the Windows NT operating system from Microsoft Corporation that looks and feels somewhat like Microsoft Windows but is far more powerful in multitasking and computing speed of a 32-bit architecture memory access. NT has extensive networking capabilities as well as being a full 32-bit processor. Most present Windows users, however, will not be able to use NT without buying more powerful computers and becoming accustomed to its lack of object-oriented features. Many experts see Windows 2000 as the operating system of choice in future networks, although networking and efforts of Sun, Novell, to stay in the market have do not make it a sure thing. A study reports that, although Hewlett-Packard would rather stay entirely in its popular UNIX networking operating system, the company recognises Windows 2000 as such a threat to UNIX that Hewlett-Packard is also expanding its operating system to include Windows 2000. According

the HP's CEO, '...three or four years down the road, NT-related systems could become significant revenue generators'.

■ Windows Cairo

a planned upgrade (scheduled for 1996) of Windows 2000 from Microsoft Corporation that will have many of the Windows Chicago object-oriented features. Cairo was originally scheduled to ship in early 1995, but in May 1994, Microsoft Corporation announced that it would be delayed due to efforts to complete

Daytona, the second release on Windows 2000.

■ **Windows Chicago**

the significant Version 4.0 upgrade of Windows to Windows 95 in year 1995. This was later upgraded to Windows 98 in 1998. Windows Chicago, Windows 95 and Windows Version 4.0 are synonyms for the first version of Windows attempting to free itself from the constrains of Microsoft DOS. Details are provided in a famous magazine in the year 1996. 'Windows 95 is expected to become the next major operating system for the mainstream desktop and portable PC'. Between now and the time most users are using forthcoming native software designed for Windows Chicago (later called Windows 95), users may efficiently run their old 16-bit Windows applications on Chicago's operating system. Windows Chicago is a 32-bit multitasking operating system that satisfies a wider array of users than either Windows 3.1 or DOS. Microsoft spent millions of dollars studying how to make Windows Chicago easier to operate than its predecessors. It is designed to be a plug and play system with enhanced features for hardware set-up and multimedia device operations. It also has Internet utilities but is not the full networking operating system of Windows 2000 that will eventually become the most widespread operating system in the world according to many analysts. At the end of 1993, there were over 40 million Windows 3.1 users as compared with 4 million OS/2 adopters and 250,000 adopters of the new Windows 2000 32-bit processors. Since Windows 2000 and even OS/2 are not well suited to most of the existing 386 and 486 computers in the world, Windows Chicago fills a big market niche until users replace older machines with higher speed and higher memory capacity PCs. However, it is reported that Microsoft will have to compromise on some of its 32-bit system promises for Chicago in order to allow the system to be squeezed into customer machines that only have 4Mb of RAM. This is the classical problem of having to compromise power of an operating system for hardware limitations of a large customer base. As a result, Windows Chicago may suffer from the same crashing problems as Windows and still be confined to 16-bit graphical device interfaces (GDI). However, experts deny that Chicago will have crashing problems. Whether or not Windows Chicago is truly better than the IBM and Apple competition operating systems may be a moot point if there are over 40 million Windows users that have installed or soon will install Windows Chicago. Market share determines the number of native software applications being developed for operating systems. Mac, UNIX and other operating systems are losing the native software development war to

Windows Chicago and Windows 2000. Windows Chicago is almost certain to become the PC operating system standard of choice until its upgrade called Windows Cairo rolls off the line and/or Windows 2000 with upgraded object-oriented programming features become the operating systems of choice among users having newer hardware speed and memory components

■ Windows daytona

see Windows 2000

■ Windows DNA

Windows Distributed Internet Applications bundling of Windows 2000, Host Integration Server 2000, Application Centre 2000, BizTalk Server 2000, Commerce Server 2000, SQL Server 2000, Internet Security and Acceleration Server 2000 and Visual Studio 2000. Microsoft hopes that many companies will soon tire of integrating best-of-breed products and will opt for an integrated solution. That's why the software vendor is preparing to release the components that make up its Windows DNA 2000 product group. see **Windows 2000**.

■ Windows Scripting Host (WSH)

see **ActiveX**.

■ Windows XP

a significant revision (code named Whistler) of the entire Windows operating system from Microsoft Corporation. Windows XP is built on the Windows 2000 kernel but brings a nee look to the desktop that will also make it easier for users to scan or import images and to acquire music files on the Web and transfer them to portable devices. The new Windows will allow different users to have their own private sets of files. The Start Menu has been redesigned to make the most-used programs easiest to find. Windows XP will come in a Professional version and a Home Edition version.. More importantly, Windows XP is more stable than Windows 2000 and Windows NT. As the Windows platform continues to evolve to address changing business computing needs, many organisations currently on UNIX platforms are turning to Windows to run their new client and server business applications. They're discovering that moving to the Windows platform does not require abandoning existing investments in UNIX applications and infrastructure.

■ WINTEL

contraction of Windows and Intel. The hardware and software combination of an Intel CPU running

Microsoft Windows. Often used with the word 'platform' in opposition to the UNIX or Macintosh platforms. Sometimes used in a derogatory sense to connote the monopoly powers that Intel and Microsoft yield.

■ wired

1. the state of being connected.
2. capitalised: a popular magazine that caters to the digerati.

■ Wireless communications

new wireless and mobile technologies. The Future of the E-Wireless Revolution Watch out, Asia and North America! Europe is defining message-delivery models for the years to come and quite possibly could become the e-wireless leader. Many web marketers are looking at the wireless web frenzy, wondering how they can jump aboard the hype train.

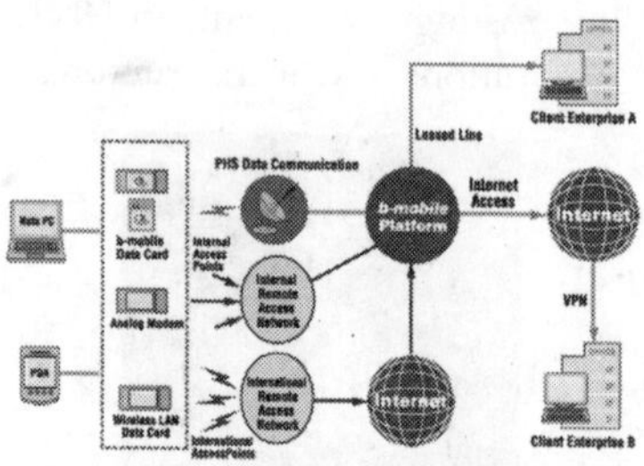

■ Wireless Local Network (WLAN)

a local area network that is not connected by wires but instead uses one of the wireless technologies.

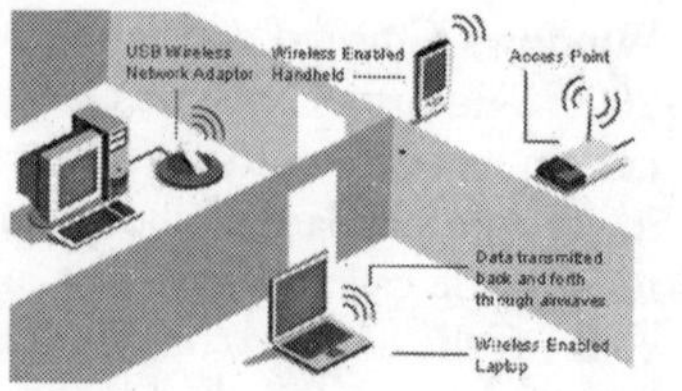

■ wizard

1. a software routine that allows for easy 'yes or no' answers to configuration, installation and set-up questions.
2. someone who is adept at making computers perform their 'magic'.

■ wizzywig

see **WYSIWYG**.

■ word variants

different word endings (such as -*ing*, *-s*, *es*, *-ism*, *-ist*,etc.) will be retrieved only if you allow for them in your search terms. One way to do this Truncation, but few systems accept truncation. Another way is to enter the variants either separated by Boolean Or (and grouped in parentheses). In +Require/-Reject non-Boolean systems, enter the variant terms preceded with neither + nor -, because this will allow documents containing any of them to retrieved.

■ work factor

the amount of work an attacker must perform to overcome security measures.

■ workstation

a networked personal computing device with more power than a traditional PC or Mac, although the term 'workstation' is now used somewhat loosely to describe any site performing complex tasks such as an Amiga video workstation, a Mac AV workstation, a CD-ROM recording workstation, a videodisc recording workstation, a desktop publishing workstation, etc. Typically, a 'workstation' has operating systems such as Unix, OS/2 or Windows 2000 that are capable of running several tasks (multitasking) at the same time. It has several megabytes of memory and a large, high-resolution display. Examples are SUN workstations and Digital DEC stations.

■ world wide web

a distributed hypertext system invented by Tim Berners-Lee on a NeXT Computer. Currently, one of the most popular services offered on the Internet. Web pages are viewed using browsing software like Netscape Navigator, Sun Microsystems Hot Java or Microsoft Internet Explorer. see also **browser, Hypertext Markup Language**.

■ WORM

Write Once Read Many depicts a write-once-read-many memory device that allows an author to store prepared files once into memory so that other users may read but not alter those files. Alternately WORM also depicts a computer program which replicates itself. The Internet worm was perhaps the most famous, it successfully duplicated itself on many of the systems across the Internet. More commonly, however, the term refers to WORM Drives such as CD-ROM recorders that will allow authors to record computer files one time on a compact disc but will not allow revisions or other materials to be added to the disc at a later time. Of course, it is often possible to download WORM files into hard drive discs and make revisions that can then be recorded on a new compact disc. The term WORM now has a somewhat bad connotation since so many destructive viruses transmitted over the e-mail and the Internet are WORM viruses.

■ WPA

Wi-fi Protected Access. An interim security standard for wireless networks designed to be more secure than WEP. It is taken from the draft 802.11i standard.

■ wrapper

a Java applet designed to display XML content embedded in traditional HTML documents. The XML contents may either be authored into the HTML document explicitly (as when the XML is authored concurrently with the HTML document) or the XML content may be unknown implicit (as when the XML document is imported). In the first case it may be beneficial for the XML elements to inherit the style properties of the parent HTML document (e.g. via. Inheritance from the parent style properties or ID and CLASS attributes), in the second case the XML content should probably be 'hidden' from the parent document. There may be multiple XML documents within the HTML document. A wrapper may use one or more 'extractors' to extract data from unstructured XML files. Extractors utilise dictionaries to achieve sophisticated linguistic processing of unstructured text. Life is much easier for structured documents having XML markups. Note that the issue of using an XML wrapper is quite different from using an XML compliant browser. One such wrapper uses <XMLDOC> tags. In XML, a tag beginning with the sequence XML is not allowed as these tags are reserved. XMLDOC however is not an XML tag it is an HTML tag.

Related to a wrapper is the concept of an XML 'extractor' for generating XML from HTML documents and databases having no XML markups. In building a XML markups, we need to provide a way for the tool to generate XML documents from existing data sources. XML markup assembly is a process of locating data (e.g., product attributes) in repositories and merging them into an XML structure that is consistent with the some predefined schema. Asset repositories can be of various types (databases, file systems, etc.) and the details of how information is retrieved from them may differ considerably. Life is much easier if the data sources have a fixed document type definition (DTD).

writing for new audiences

authorware 4 has been substantially retooled for Web deployment and functionality. It now supports external content controls, so a completed project can reference external media elements on a LAN, an intranet or the Internet. This lets you develop a program that can be updated without having to rebuild the entire project, simply update the media that the program references. Of course, you must manage these external files religiously and if used in the final project, path name relationships must remain constant.

External links are managed through the aptly named External Media Browser, an essential new tool that lets you track external media efficiently and relatively painlessly.

Authorware titles can be played across the Web using Macromedia Shockwave technology. Unlike Director 6, Authorware still requires you to run a project through a separate Afterburner utility (included with the program) to 'shock' it for the Web.

Version 4 adds support for a number of file formats, including GIF, JPEG and Adobe Photoshop. Images can be resized and cropped within the development environment, allowing for considerable flexibility in the process.

The program also adds a collection of Quickstart templates to help beginners create typical interactive projects.

Authorware is fully cross-platform, but there are minor differences between the two versions. Most significant is that the Mac version doesn't support Microsoft ActiveX controls, while the PC version does. This is less the fault of Macromedia than of Microsoft Corp., which has been slow to bring ActiveX technology to the Mac. Still, it's a significant issue for cross-platform developers who want to use the technology.

Despite the program's otherwise unsurpassed text-handling capabilities (including support for style sheet and RTF text import), Authorware still does not offer anti-aliased text—a serious omission. Director, which is less aimed at text-based programs, has offered this feature since Version 5.0. We hope Macromedia fixes this rather annoying problem.

While the interface is generally improved, Authorware still relies too much on dialog boxes. You often have to tunnel through several layers of them to change a single characteristic.

■ WRT

abbreviation for With Respect To.

■ W-vhs

see **Wide-screen TV.**

■ x.25

an international standard for packet switching, typically used with older telephone networks for data communications.

■ x.400

e-mail protocol developed by the CCITT and endorsed by the ISO as part of the OSI protocol family.

■ x.500

a directory access protocol to enable a common standard for directories of information over a network. It has never caught on as well as its designers intended.

■ x.509

Public key certificate specification developed as part of the X.500 directory specification and often used in public key systems.

■ XBRL

Extensible Business Reporting Language. This is an extension of XML metatag technology key terminologies in business, accounting and financial reporting. The major purpose is to allow users to locate and analyse financial reports or portions of financial reports in a manner that is far more efficient and effective than using traditional search engines and EDGAR utilities.

The main starting point in understanding XBRL is the XBRL Home Page.

XBRL is a standards-based method with which users can prepare, publish in a variety of formats, exchange and analyse financial statements and the information they contain.

Licensed royalty-free worldwide by XBRL International, a non-profit consortium consisting of over 140 leading companies, associations and government agencies around the world.

Permits the automatic exchange and reliable extraction of financial information across all software formats and technologies, including the Internet.

Benefits all users of the financial information supply chain: public and private companies, the accounting profession, regulators, analysts, the investment community, capital markets and lenders, as well as key third parties such as software developers and data aggregators.

Does not require a company to disclose any additional information beyond that which they normally disclose under existing accounting standards.

Does not require a change to existing accounting standards.

Improves access to financial information by improving the form of the information and making it more appropriate for the Internet.

Reduces the need to enter financial information more than one time, reducing the risk of data entry error and eliminating the need to manually key information for various formats, (printed financial statement, an HTML document for a company's Web site, an EDGAR filing document, a raw XML file or other specialised reporting formats such as credit reports and loan documents) thereby lowering a company's cost to prepare and distribute its financial statements while improving investor or analyst access to information.

Leverages efficiencies of the Internet as today's primary source of financial information. More than 80% of major US public companies provide some type of financial disclosure on the Internet and the majority of information that investors use to make decisions comes to them via the Internet.

XBRL meets the needs of today's investors and other users of financial information by providing accurate and reliable information to help them make informed financial decisions.

Note that early in the Year 2000, XFRML at the American Institute of Certified Public Accountants had a name change to XBRL.

Efforts are underway to create standards for a new Dynamic HTML (DHTML) in a Document Object Model (DOM). However, progress is slow. A problem with DHTML is that it is inefficient and requires too many scripts to perform simple tasks. Moving beyond DHTML is Extensible Markup Language (XML) originating with Goldfarb and Bosak for putting tags on web pages to facilitate more efficient web searches. The XML term is misnamed in the sense that it is not technically a markup language. XML is becoming popular for business operations and web sites.

■ XHTML

a variant of HTML. Stands for Extensible Hypertext Markup Language is a hybrid between HTML and XML that is more universally acceptable in Web pages and search engines than XML.

■ XML

Extensible Markup Language, a dilution for Web page use of SGML

(Standard General Markup Language), which is not readily viewable in ordinary browsers and is difficult to apply to Web pages. XML is very useful (among other things) for pages emerging from databases and other applications where parts of the page are standardised and must reappear many times. see **XHTML**.

■ XMLRPC

XML Remote Procedure Call. A protocol for client-server communication that sends and receives information on top of HTTP. The data sent and received is in a particular *XML* format specifically designed for use with XMLRPC.

■ xmodem

an early form of file transmission for dialup and telnet connections. It is slower and uses smaller blocks of data (128 bits) than ymodem and zmodem.

■ XPFE

Cross Platform Front End. A suite of technologies used to create applications that will work and look the same on different computer operating systems. A widely used XPFE application is the Mozilla web browser and its derivities, such as the Netscape web browser in version 7 and later. The primary technologies used in creating XPFE applications are Javascript, Cascading Style Sheets and XUL.

■ XSL

Extensible Scripting Language. An XML style sheet language supported by the newer web browsers Internet Explorer 5 and Netscape 5.

■ XUL

Extensible User-Interface Language. A markup language similar to HTML and based on XML.
XUL used to define what the user interface will look like for a particular piece of software. XUL is used to define what buttons, scrollbars, text boxes and other user-interface items will appear, but it is not used to define how those item will look (e.g. what colour they are).
The most widely used example of XUL use is probably in the Mozilla web browser, where the entire user interface is defined using the XUL language.

■ Yahoo

similar to a search engine, but with a database generated by hand, this is the world's most used directory of web sites. The main URL is http://www.yahoo.com. It is notoriously difficult to get listed in Yahoo and, once listed, even more difficult to get your listing changed or to get out! To increase the odds of getting listed, try the following:

Select the three categories you want to be listed in very carefully. Consider the regional categories. Ensure that the categories match the content of your site.

Apply to one of their local subsidiaries for your own country or city.

Make sure that your site is well-designed and easy to navigate.

Ensure your site has no dead links.

Ensure that your pages download quickly.

Provide good contact information on your site.

If you manage to get listed, keep the e-mail they send you. You can e-mail the same person subsequently to get your listing changed.

■ YMMV

abbreviation of 'Your Mileage May Vary', taken from the standard disclaimer attached to EPA mileage ratings. This warning can be found in some UNIX freeware distributions.

■ ymodem

a common form of file transmission for dialup and telnet connections, which uses 1K blocks of data. It has two forms- single file mode and batch mode. The single file form is sometimes called 1K xmodem and the batch mode is sometimes called ymodem batch. Usage is not consistent. Zmodem is newer and more reliable.

■ Z39.50

'American National Standard Z39.50: Information Retrieval Service Definition and Protocol Specification for Library Applications'. This was designed to be a standard for connecting library computers and databases regardless of hardware and software. It could be used as a standard for many kinds of databases. It has not caught on and there are many, many other database protocols in use today in and out of libraries.

■ zip

a method of file compression originally used with MSDOS and a file extension for files which are zip compressed.

■ zmodem

a very common form of file transmission, which can be used across dialup and telnet connections. It can be used in batch modes (for multiple files) and it is faster than the older xmodem and ymodem. In some implementations, it can resume a transfer after a connection has been broken and re-established.

■ zulu time

zulu time, often used in US Government communications, is another way of saying Greenwich Mean Time (GMT).

■ zup?

chat shorthand for 'What'z up?'.